Mastering
SELF-CARE

*Building Resiliency through Healthy
and Mindful Living*

Carol,

So blessed to be journeying
with you! Thank you
for all your help along
the way. Love always,
Suzie

Rev. Suzie DeVaughn, LMSW

PAGE PUBLISHING, INC.
Conneaut Lake, PA

First originally published by Page Publishing 2021

ISBN 978-1-6624-3020-6 (pbk)
ISBN 978-1-6624-3021-3 (digital)

Printed in the United States of America

I dedicate this book to the many who will be reading it, with the hope that you take your worthiness of excellent health into your heart. May you be inspired to reach for the stars and know that anything is possible!

Acknowledgments

I would like to express the deepest gratitude for the amazing people in my life who made this book possible. A special thank-you to my father, who first encouraged me to share my story and the wisdom I gained through writing this book. And to my mother, who was a great support when she was alive and still supports me from the other side. To my children, who love me unconditionally and inspire me to help make this world a better place, for they and the other youth are the future. To my sister-in-law, who was a great cheerleader in keeping me on point as I wrote and made several passes through to provide feedback. To my brother, who helped me get Self-Care Specialists going in the early days. Thank you to Kathy Figley of Figley Institute for helping me to get started with permission to use her training slides and workbook. My immense appreciation goes to several dear friends, you know who you are, who provided feedback and editing assistance before I turned it over to Page Publishing. My heartfelt gratitude goes out to all the healers and lightworkers, too many to mention, who helped me through my healing journey. My life would not be what it is today without you, and the service I provide would not be possible without the healing that occurred between us.

Contents

Preface

Although my initial work began with the focus of bringing awareness of the importance of self-care to caregivers as it pertained to the professionals in the medical and mental health fields, first responders, animal caregivers, and educators, this book is written for everyone. We are all caregivers of someone whether it is within our professions, as parents, grandparents, intimate partners, pet lovers, friends, and others. As adults, we are caregivers of ourselves, responsible for meeting our needs in every way. According to Maslow's hierarchy of needs, these include physiological, safety, love/belongingness, esteem, and self-actualization.[1] Our self-care is of the utmost importance and is each individual's responsibility. What we need is a self-care movement in which each person loves, cares, and takes responsibility for one's self. By acknowledging and responding to our needs, we have more energy and compassion to help others. In this scenario everyone benefits.

Through research, self-care has been discovered to be the greatest prevention of secondary stress-related traumas in professional caregivers. It helps to increase the resiliency necessary to counterbalance the stress encountered in demanding and high-burnout profes-

Figure 1. Maslow's hierarchy of needs

---

[1] Saul McLeod, "Maslow's Hierarchy of Needs," March 20, 2020, accessed August 2020, https://www.simplypsychology.org/maslow.html.

sions. The metaphor of putting on your oxygen mask before helping others to put on theirs is relevant here. In order to provide excellent service to others, we must be at a place of optimum wellness and functioning. Otherwise, it depletes our reserves and can eventually lead to compassion fatigue, secondary traumatic stress, vicarious traumatization, and burnout.

I do not see this to be much different for the general public, to all of us. In this day and age, stress is on the rise. There is much turmoil as our society is struggling to find its way into peace and community, a rebirth of sorts. It is not pretty, but hopefully many people wake up to the destruction we are doing to ourselves, others, and the planet by lacking awareness. Sometimes things must deconstruct before they can be rebuilt. We are microcosms of the whole, and many of us are going through difficult transitions and awakenings. Sometimes the messages get really loud until we hear them.

The message for many is to take better care of ourselves. We get the message through pain, deteriorating health, feeling depleted of energy, anxiety, depression, hopelessness, and beyond. The increased reliance on medications and medical treatment is an indication that many people are not getting healthier. Some want a pill to make it all better, yet the pills have side effects and often treat the symptoms rather than the root of the problem.

The root of the problem can usually be found within ourselves and our lifestyle choices. These include the food we eat, the substances we consume, poor habits, chemical exposure, self-destructive patterns, our negative or restrictive thoughts and beliefs, unresolved emotions and traumas, continuous exposure to stress, and beyond. Some of the problems result from the bigger picture—environmental pollutants in the air we breathe, the water we drink, the quality of the soil our food is grown in and more. A portion of this is unavoidable until global solutions appear, yet much of this we can influence. For the sake of this book, let us focus on the things we can influence.

I encourage you to read this book with an open mind. It may not all resonate with you, but hopefully there are some things you can take into your current self-care practice or you will find the inspiration to begin a self-care regimen. I encourage you to meet yourself where you are, without judgment. Self-care is a practice that can always be deepened, but we must start where we are. It may seem overwhelming if you try to do too much at once, and this can lead to defeat before getting started. A gentle, curious approach is recommended. You did not get where you are in a day, and it will not be resolved in a day. I invite you to focus on progress, not perfection.

I am sure that nothing I share in this book is new, and it has all been said before. I share from my perspective, experiences, and training. It has been a journey that forced me into excellent self-care practices for survival. Like you, I have had my struggles—many of them. These struggles were gifts that set me on a path of self-care practices that have changed my life and allowed me to assist many others to improve their lives. It took a strong commitment to my self-care, a true investment in myself, and a lot of deep inner work to reap the rewards.

The greatest gift you have to offer the world is yourself. You are unique, perfect in your imperfection, and filled with light at your core. By taking excellent care of your body, mind, and soul, you can peel away the inauthentic layers of yourself and discover more of who you are. When we give to ourselves, we have more to give others. It is an inside job, and your world starts within *you* and radiates out!

I begin this book by sharing my story, giving you an insight into some of the experiences that have brought me to a place of proficiency with self-care. I will discuss self-care as a foundation for wellness and how to make space for more self-care in your life. Multiple dimensions of self-care will be presented including physical self-care, psychological self-care, interpersonal self-care, professional self-care, and spiritual self-care. Infused within these dimensions are ideas of things you can do to and for yourself to improve your self-care regimen. I will discuss energy management and clearing methods, which is particularly helpful for highly empathic individuals. Included is a chapter regarding secondary trauma and special considerations for professional caregivers. Self-assessments on a variety of subjects are included to encourage self-reflection. Finally, I will finish by discussing how to put ideas into action with self-care strategy.

> Disclaimer: This information is presented for educational purposes only. It is not a substitute for informed medical advice or training. Do not use this information to diagnose or treat health problems without consulting a qualified health or mental health provider. If you have concerns, contact your health-care provider or mental health professional.

CHAPTER 1

My Story

We delight in the beauty of the butterfly, but rarely admit the changes it has gone through to achieve that beauty.
—Maya Angelou,
American poet and author
(Goodreads.com)

My journey into self-care began in 1996, nearly twenty-five years ago, when I had unknowingly exposed myself to arsenic through the usage of bug bombs and pesticides. My husband at the time and I chose to utilize bug bombs in our home to save money, as we had just built a house and were nearly overextended financially. Living in the state of Kansas, a home of the brown recluse spiders and with a shake shingle roof where they loved to reside, we were trying to keep our home free of the poisonous spiders. We both lacked awareness regarding the harmful effects of the bug bombs and what they were made with. Our thought was that if it was approved to be sold in mainstream stores within the United States, it must be okay. Additionally, my in-laws had their home and trees sprayed with pesticides often so that we could enjoy the fire at night without getting bug bites. We often took walks on our neighborhood golf course, which was also heavily sprayed with chemicals to maintain its aesthetic appeal.

During that time, I began having migraine headaches and upper respiratory problems, something that I had never experienced before. Our family physician diagnosed the cause as sinus infections, and I was sent to a pulmonary specialist, who diagnosed me with asthma. I was given prescription pain medication for the migraines, seven rounds of antibiotics, a few rounds of steroids, inhalers, and oral asthma medications. Despite the usage of the antibiotics and steroids, things were not getting better. In fact, there were a host of other problems developing within my body. These included digestive problems of discomfort and bloating and continuous flu-like symptoms and fatigue. I became severely hypoglycemic and was losing weight even though I ate a lot, resulting in becoming underweight. Sleep was compromised for years, ranging from light restless sleep to insomnia. There was a period of time in which I only slept an hour to two per night (on a good night) for an entire year. My nervous system was severely compromised. I became allergic to every inhalant allergy tested for and many foods, to the point where the list of choices was small. You get the idea; my health was seriously deteriorating.

After multiple visits to a variety of medical doctors and specialists, none could figure out what was wrong with me. The doctors could do little to help and often referred me to yet another doctor, with no understanding of the problem or relief of my symptoms. I became distrusting of their ability to help, noticing that when prescribed medications, my symptoms worsened. Depression and hopelessness set in, and it seemed like I would never get better. I had even considered suicide as it seemed there was no end in sight after years of suffering.

It was time to turn to holistic health care, a concept that was new to me and not very accepted in Kansas at the time. It took trying a few practitioners before finding the right fit. This put a strain on my marriage because my husband highly regarded the medical profession and believed that chiropractic, kinesiology, acupuncture treatments, and the like were "snake oil." Although finding relief through sublingual allergy drops, proper supplementation, regular chiropractic/kinesiology appointments, and lifestyle changes, he was not able to support me on this alternative path of healing.

With the proper resources and my personal commitment to clean living and diligent self-care, I began recovering after seven years of suffering. My self-care had become extreme. My diet evolved to eating organic foods (pesticide, steroid/hormone free, preservative free, no food colorings, etc.), following Barry Sears' the Zone diet consisting of lean protein, good fats, and low-glycemic carbohydrates to regulate hormones (it healed my blood-sugar issues, and I returned to a healthy weight) and gluten-free foods. Sugar, dairy, yeast, and alcohol were eliminated. I went green and got chemicals out of the home and off the yard.

My new norm included the mind-body exercises of Pilates and yoga, as well as daily walks. I began a meditation practice and enjoyed breath work. Regular appointments with my kinesiologist/chiropractor were continued as maintenance. Doing work with a therapist helped me overcome trauma from the health crisis and to heal the many other things we found that I needed to work on. The lifestyle I was leading was considered very alternative at the time, especially in the middle of Kansas.

My health finally seemed on track, and we were blessed with three healthy children. I had the pleasure of staying home and raising them until they were all in school. The ten years home with them were deeply satisfying and healing, as I had time to nurture them and myself. It gave my body, mind, and soul the space it needed to heal.

On Christmas Day of 2003, at the age of fifty-six, my mother lost her life to a twelve-year battle with breast cancer. I felt too young to lose my mother at the age of thirty-four with a four-year-old and a six-month-old baby. She was a dear friend and an amazing influence.

In 2009, when the kids were three, five, and eight years old, my husband and I decided to separate and eventually divorce. We were growing apart in interests and lifestyle and decided to set each other free to experience life the way we each preferred.

Prior to our decision to separate, I had been accepted into graduate school at Wichita State University to pursue my master's in social work. My husband agreed to support myself and the children throughout graduate school, allowing me to follow my dreams. He followed his dream of opening a law firm. I realized I was walking away from the financial stability of his successful adventure. Venturing into the unknown by entering graduate school and becoming a single parent at the age of forty was a big and bold change.

The decision to divorce was terrifying and exhilarating. We married right out of college when he was in law school. I had not even paid bills, as he handled the finances. A host of emotions came with this transition as well, as more were triggered from my parents' divorce at the age of five. The deep therapy work was most fascinating and freeing as I discovered and released skeletons from the closet of the past that were beneath my awareness. With each session came increased freedom, self-empowerment, and more compassion for myself.

I completed graduate school in three years, graduating in May of 2012. It was an intense time period with three young children, healing myself and the children from the pain caused by the divorce, coursework, practicum years, and picking up over 320 hours of out-of-state classroom psychotherapy training hours in Boulder, Colorado, and various parts of California. This was the beginning of an interesting path, which included public speaking and assisting others on their healing journeys.

Doors opened that utterly amazed and humbled me. My first year of practicum was at a holistic health center—right up my alley! I went to fifteen different social-service agencies, proposing to develop and deliver a program for the participants of their organizations. Each social-service leader I met said their social workers, therapists, and mental health professionals really needed the assistance. I had been researching self-care as treatment and prevention of secondary trauma in professional caregivers. My great passion for self-care was married with a population that was most in need of my knowledge and service. It seemed like a match made in heaven! I created and delivered over twenty presentations on mindfulness meditation and nutrition. I organized and co-facilitated several trainings on acupressure for stress relief with the owner/acupuncturist of the holistic health center. At this time, during 2010 in Kansas, most of them had not heard of or experienced meditation. It gave me great joy to share something that had become an important part of my life and healing.

The second year of practicum I worked at the same holistic health center and within a women's shelter delivering therapy services. Additionally, I facilitated a self-care group with the social workers at the women's shelter. My studies included Hakomi body-centered psychotherapy, EMDR, and Psych-K in out-of-state training workshops with the intention of hitting the ground running upon graduation. It seemed there was no time to waste as I was beginning my second career at the age of forty-four.

Following graduation in May of 2012, I took time off, which eventually became six months, to rejuvenate following such an intense time of study. I was physically exhausted and needed time to recover from what seemed like a mountain that I had just climbed. Serious self-care, self-nurturing, and time with my children was needed. Clarity regarding my career was necessary and knowing that if I got clear within myself, the Universe would assist. In my mind, my options were doing therapy in a private practice or in community mental health. Neither option resonated with me, but I was not sure what the other options were. Regardless, I needed to do some inner work, rejuvenate, and rebalance.

During this time, I did some subconscious belief repatterning regarding my goals, which removed the blockages for the next phase of my life. Working with a mentor who used a modality I had just learned, Psych-K subconscious repatterning, my goals focused on health, career, and personal development. These goals are based on the premise that when you believe it to be true both consciously and subconsciously and take action toward living in your truth, it will manifest *as* your truth. This will become your reality in the physical world. The goals I balanced for each did come true in their own special timing and way. They are as follows:

- I am perfectly healthy on all levels. (I thought I was healthy, but did it as "insurance," more on this later as it paved the way for additional healing, which made it a true reality.)
- I am happy that I have the perfect job/environment fit where work feels like play and is natural.

- I am thrilled to have a job with flexible work hours that accommodate the kids' schedules, my self-care, travel, and other personal needs.
- I am fortunate to have an employer located close to my home.
- I attract clients with a genuine desire for growth and healing.
- I am valued for speaking my truth and feel free to be me at work each and every day.
- I am thrilled that I have a position that allows me to serve the highest and best of the client, agency, community, and the planet.

In January of 2013, I got clear on what I was to do, and it was not an option that I'd ever considered. After preparing my taxes with a new level of confidence, I heard this message as if it came from outside myself, "Now you can start your business." At first, there was resistance as I did not believe I had the knowledge and ability to start my own business. Then recalling my days in the corporate world and realizing I had just done a pilot experience while in graduate school practicum doing presentations and therapy made it seem more realistic.

I began a business called Self-Care Specialists, which would deliver care for the caregiver. A relationship with Dr. Kathy Regan Figley, president of Figley Institute, was developed. Kathy's husband, Dr. Charles Figley, is a leading researcher regarding secondary trauma and its prevention with self-care. In fact, he coined the term *compassion fatigue* in 1995. With their research and the portion of their training utilized (with their permission) and my experience, I put an amazing workshop together. A portion of their training was incorporated for a year before making the training my own, with reference to a few of their slides and studies. I became an approved continuing-education provider with Kansas State Behavioral Sciences Board, Kansas Board of Nursing, and Kansas Board of Emergency Medical Services. I offered Compassion Stress Management, Self-Care Is Ethical Practice, and Mindfulness in Practice full-day training workshops for professional caregivers. Through these workshops, the professional caregivers (including mental health professionals, medical professionals, emergency responders, animal caregivers, and educators) were able to get continuing education toward their re-licensure where appropriate and approved.

Additionally, I began offering psychotherapy in my home office with a clientele of primarily professional caregivers and entrepreneurs utilizing the deep body-centered and mindfulness-based psychotherapy modalities learned while in school. All the career goals previously mentioned came true, although it looked different than imagined. I became my own boss, worked in my home rather than close to home (even better!), and was able to speak my truth in a bigger way than expected through public speaking.

While laying the foundation for my business, I did some deep-tissue body work called the Rolfing Method of Structural Integration of approximately twenty-five sessions over a six-month time period. I began to feel the frighteningly familiar flu-like symptoms and overwhelming fatigue experienced many years back during the health crisis. During chiropractic/kinesiology appointments, my practitioner kept picking up that it was due to heavy metals.

Following some research, I was led to a healer who does Chinese medicine, acupuncture, chiropractic, and kinesiology. Additionally, he had healed from debilitating illness involving heavy metal toxicity thirty years ago. I knew from my personal journey that some of the best, most compassionate healers had to heal themselves. During the first appointment, he identified the problem through kinesiology muscle testing. I had arsenic in my kidneys, liver, and my lymphatic system was congested. Additionally, my kidneys, liver, and adrenals were not functioning well.

Having lost faith in traditional Western medicine, I had several appointments with this alternative doctor and a holistic MD who practiced functional medicine. They both agreed that prescription chelation therapy and herbal organ support was necessary to assist my body in getting the toxins out and that it would take a miracle. One even argued with me on how that miracle would occur. I told him, "I will get the miracle through the power of my belief." After rounds of arguing, I said, "Let's get back to why I am here...you are my doctor, not my minister. Sit back and watch...I will receive the miracle."

After six months of rigorous oral chelation therapy and expensive herbal organ support, I weaned myself off, against the advice of my primary doctor. It had helped, but something was still wrong and should have felt better after the large amount of toxins had been released from my body. I reached out to a professional intuitive from the past and received the message that it would take a miracle and I had done everything medically possible. She said I may only have a few years to live and that the only way I would get the miracle would be through spirit. I was very frustrated as I had been praying and connecting with my Divine daily and keeping myself in a space of unconditional love and positivity most of the time. Here is an entry from my journal, written on November 4, 2014.

> November 4, 2014—The chemical healing program I have been taking through Dr. L has cost thousands of dollars, and it is beyond my financial means at this time. Although I believe it has helped me, I am frustrated with the routine of taking so many herbs, supplements, and two chelators twice a day. Something is still wrong. I woke feeling a bit toxic today, but regardless decided to stop taking everything but a few supplements. Today is the day I surrender my healing to spirit. I do not want to further congest my body with supplements. It is a little scary but freeing. Although he says there is still arsenic in my body, I am trusting spirit to purify me of that, other impurities and of the herbs/supplements. Today is a day of letting go, renewal, and rebirth. I have no idea what will happen but letting go and surrendering is part of my journey. If spirit cannot do this, no one can. I have important work to do on this planet and trust that if I am to

do it, spirit will find a way. My plan is to further purify myself through my connection to source, daily meditation, daily green smoothies, diet, and light exercise. I have read stories about people who experienced miraculous healing, even from diseases like cancer, through prayer and positive thinking. I recall hoping that I would never have an experience that tested my faith to the point of having to heal through prayer and positive thinking, although I've had a sense that such an experience would be part of my path. It scared me because I did not know if I'd ever be strong enough to conquer such a challenge. Indeed, such an opportunity has arrived. Since I learned of the arsenic, I have had a knowing that I chose this as part of my path for the good of humanity and that I could educate others on self-healing by going through the experience.

November 28, 2014—To catch up from my last entry, getting off my chelators and organ support did not go so well. I discontinued them for just one full day and started to feel horrible. My nervous system was struggling, my lymphatic system became sluggish and my urination became minimal. It was obvious to me that I had to keep taking the support and chelation therapy. Although I felt done with the arsenic, it was not done with me. I had had two professional intuitives, Cynthia and Julia, tell me to get off the herbs/supplements. Julia had told me through readings that I could detox naturally and that the supplements were congesting my body. She also told me that the arsenic was gone. Cynthia told me to get off the supplements and that no one doctor could help me. She said I may only have a few years to live, that it would take a miracle and that the healing would come through spirit. I do not doubt that it will take a miracle, but I believe in miracles and know that I will get mine. In the meantime, I will keep taking my organ support and chelators as it is obvious that they are helping me right now. I would have to find a way to continue my therapy—and pray for a miracle!

December 5, 2014—I went to see Dr. L to get straightened out. I was dumping a lot of arsenic identified through kinesiology testing. I felt gratitude for his assistance. I also felt stuck, like there was no easy way out of this predicament or to heal it.

December 6, 2014—I had a breakdown in my bed this evening. I sobbed uncontrollably and spoke with God, more like yelled. I called in my angels, guides, ascended masters, such as Jesus, Buddha, Kwan Yin, Mother Mary, and Arch Angel Raphael to help. I confessed I was afraid, as I had many times before, and had no idea how to heal the situation. I pleaded for a miracle and promised in return to dedicate my life to the service of others. I would need energy and healing to do all that I had set out to accomplish on this earthly plane. I also surrendered to the fact that perhaps I was not supposed to make it through this, and if so, would be of limited service as my days passed. After I'd exhausted myself from sobbing, I heard a voice that said, "Now we can help you." I went in to take a bath. While in the tub, I heard a voice, which I believed to be Jesus, that said, "Don't be afraid." After all, this sounded like something Jesus would say. I had a feeling something was coming that would be a little scary, but the assurance made me excited to see what the message was about. I put in a movie to watch in my bed. I could not breathe, which was not uncommon when I was dumping arsenic. It seemed more intense. I felt tired of fighting for breath and just stopped trying. I turned off the movie, rolled onto my back, and shut my eyes. I stopped trying to breathe and allowed my breath to slow. It eventually slowed to what felt like approximately one breath per minute. This went on for an estimated hour. It felt as if I could stop breathing and just let go. My body was stiff and getting cold. I was unable to move. My consciousness remained, although my body seemed to be fading. I was not afraid and felt a surrender. Then I received the message: "You can stay or peacefully go; it is your choice." I very objectively thought about three things…my children, the beloved partner I had not yet met yet, and the service I was here to offer. The objectivity as the options were quickly considered was most unusual. I decided to stay and after several minutes attempted to open my eyes. I was able to open them and after a considerable amount of time, slowly begin moving. It seems as if spirit has begun breathing for me as I have not had shortness of breath since that day (today is 12/30). I call this my "near, near-death experience."

I reached out to another professional intuitive, someone I had heard great things about, to see what she picked up. Here are some entries from my journal:

December 19, 2014—Today I had a reading with a professional intuitive named Avianna.

My knowing regarding my situation is that I will have a full recovery and that I will heal faster and deeper than my doctors believe is possible. When anything to the contrary is said, an inner knowing and anger flare from deep within. One of my doctors, the MD, said, "The only way you will heal this is by connecting with God through Jesus Christ." We argued a bit as I have my own beliefs and connection with God. I eventually told him, "We'll have to agree to disagree and let's get back to the reason I am here." My other doctor told me I'd never heal completely and that I'd always have some arsenic in my body. If I were to believe this, then it would become my reality. Luckily, I believe in a full recovery and optimal health.

My reading with Avianna went well, and her intuitive impressions resonated with me. We did it by phone, me in Kansas and her in a distant state. She knew nothing about me except my name and phone number. I did not let her know about my business or give her my business email as that would give her some information about me. She quickly picked up on my age and that I was healing from something that happened approximately halfway through my life. Impressive as the origin of the arsenic was when I first married and was exposed to it through bug bombs and heavy pesticides used by us and his family. Not only was I healing the arsenic from that time but the heavy and negative energy from that time. She said it was a miracle, a blessing that I was still here and that my soul had come to this earthly plane with a large agenda and a lot to accomplish. She saw that I would make a full recovery and that by June of 2015, I would feel very different from today and be completely recovered by 2016. She got that I would need to take supplements and herbal support for 4–6 months and that they are helping to clear out old energy. I was given the advice to keep taking them as they are really good for me and acting like healers in my body. This resonated as I got sick when I stopped taking them. She said I am here to bring heightened awareness to people with the same situation. She said I would write more than one book, design a program to help others in the same situation, would speak in auditoriums and large places. She said eventually I would go into research mode and create a training or engineer a product or healing modality. She said people like to hear me speak because I speak truth with both strength and compassion, an unusual combination. I was told that year 2015 would be a year of release, surrender, opening and allowing and that 2016 would be my year. She said the next 6 months would be pivotal and "earth-shattering!" OMG! I just got a validation from spirit through a loud noise that came from the chandelier above where I sit. She also said that I would work through the healing and that I would not suffer. Thank goodness, as it seems I have suffered enough. It feels like I have been a dog climbing a mountain with three legs. AMEN! She also said that I will start a spiritual business. Hmmm? Not sure about that but am open to possibilities.

In February of 2015, with guidance and assistance of a professional intuitive and my former kinesiologist, in three weeks, I went from two chelators and over fifty supplements/herbs to six basic supplements. I could still feel that something was wrong and knew there had to be a better way.

During that time, a healer with a crystal-light therapy bed was doing sessions at a local spiritual bookstore. The night before my session, I began researching how the founder of the healing bed channeled positive healing energy with outstanding results. I scheduled a distant healing session with him that would take place four days later. The effect of the crystal-light therapy bed was that it felt as if I released an elephant off my chest, the heaviness and grief of the situation I had been experiencing. Later, the night before my distant healing session was to occur with the energy healer, I could see his spirit healers working on me (spirit is not limited by time and space). There were five of them, all wearing white. The one in the center, who appeared to be in charge, wore all white with a gold medallion and had a bald head. I could feel them working, especially around my liver, and it felt as if there was a probe going into it. Then I fell sleep and woke the next day feeling as if something had happened. I was very tired, made breakfast, and went back to bed for the day. The next week was much the same.

Having concern about the overwhelming fatigue, I reached out to the professional intuitive who helped me wean off my treatment. She looked into the situation and started to become overwhelmed. She said she needed a few minutes because she was not sure how to convey the information she received.

I could not wait! I was so excited that I blurted out, "It's gone. The arsenic is gone, isn't it?"

She said, "Yes, it is gone, and so is the damage that it caused. The arsenic caused two tumors, one at the bottom of your right lung, and the other at the top of your liver. They had performed psychic surgery, and you got your miracle!"

I was excited yet humbled, feeling the truth of what she said. It was sobering to walk around realizing I had cancer and grateful for not knowing. She recommended that I rest for two weeks because my body was responding as if I had been in the hospital following surgery.

After a week and a half of lying around resting and sleeping, I decided to attend my Pilates class, vowing to take it slow. While driving, I got a message from one of my guides to do the "roll down."

The roll down is an exercise done on the Cadillac, a piece of equipment, in which you roll down from a sitting position one vertebrae at a time until you descend to a lying position. I had not been able to physically do this move for the past several years because it felt like something was getting caught, in the way within the right side of my body. I never thought much of it or had any concern. I realized this would be my validation, as the catching was in the area where she said the tumors were. If I could do the exercise that had not been physically possible for the past several years, it would be the validation that what I was told was true. I had a private lesson with my instructor and was able to do the roll down perfectly, without anything getting caught or hooked!

I was very fatigued following the months of chelation treatment as it took a lot out of me and left me with an electrolyte imbalance and adrenal fatigue. I took the kids to Hawaii and experienced a rebirth on my forty-sixth birthday, which had been predicted by an astrologist from Boulder several years before. I felt scrubbed by the ocean, the full moon, and planetary shifts that were taking place at the time. Upon our return, I asked my former husband to have primary care of the kids for two months to recover from the trauma I had just been through, which he graciously agreed to do. The time spent with them was less in quantity, more about quality. It was a most difficult letting go for a mother, but very necessary to get back to having the energy I needed. I felt I had nothing left to give and needed space to heal.

Something I did not anticipate was during that time I would create a new spiritual business called Blossoming Heart Center. Through this business, I would facilitate energy healing, meditations, and psychospiritual workshops. I grew so much through the difficulties that I needed another business that would allow me to expand outside the confines of my license. With the start of this new venture, new spiritual gifts also began to appear. My spirit guides gave me this message: "You had to experience the miracle to share the miracle." I have and continue to witness the miracles of my clients through the healings that I facilitate. Some examples of this will be illustrated later in the book.

I have since experienced a full recovery and have had additional validation of my healing and state of health. In September of 2018, I had a body scan done with the Biofield Viewer at an energy medicine conference, which showed that my body is doing great with an outstanding lymphatic system, healthy organs, and no sign of tumors. Additionally, it showed that all my chakras, also known as energy centers, were wide open and connected to source. I did an ionic detoxifying foot bath in June of 2019 and the practitioner indicated that in the fifteen years she administered them, she had never seen the water following the process to be as clean as mine was. This was an amazing validation, considering where I have been and how much debris these baths contained in the past. I ran into Dr. L at the health food store in August of 2020, and he was stunned at how good I looked at the age of fifty-one. In December of 2020, I did a computerized biofeedback session with a holistic practitioner that indicated my biological age to be ten based on the comprehensive factors it measured. This was another validation that my physical body, organs, systems, and cells are healthy and functioning exceptionally well.

At the age of fifty-one, I feel better than I did in my early twenties prior to the health crisis. I continue with excellent self-care and my commitment to a mindful and healthy lifestyle. It is as natural as breathing and gives me all the energy necessary to keep up with my children, their activities, my businesses, and other endeavors.

It is time to expand my services to a much larger audience, and so I write this book. I have learned much about self-care and the importance of incorporating it into daily living. My desire to share with others in hopes of inspiring or assisting them to prevent or heal from situations such as those mentioned is overwhelming. I know in my heart that my experiences have been perfect and have led me to this path of service.

CHAPTER 2

Self-Care Foundation

Caring for your body, mind and spirit is your greatest and grandest responsibility. It's about listening to the needs of your soul and then honoring them.
—**Kristi Ling,** American writer (Goodreads.com)

Defining Self-Care

Self-care is a term that has recently been become popular. *Self-care* is any "activity of an individual that is done with the intention of improving or maintaining wellness." Simply put, *self-care* is "taking care of one's wellness needs." Categories for self-care can include (1) physical—body work, exercise, adequate sleep, nutrition; (2) psychological—effective relaxation time, contact with nature, forms of creative expression, balance between work and recreation; (3) social/interpersonal—supportive relationships and knowing when/how to obtain help; and (4) professional—balancing work and home life, setting boundaries and limits, and getting help/support through peers, role models, and supervisors.[2] We'll be discussing these categories and more in the upcoming chapters.

Beliefs about Self-Care

While self-care may seem like an obvious thing to do, it is something that many of us struggle with. There has not been much emphasis on self-care societally, beyond diet and exercise, until recently, and there is still a lot of room to grow in subject awareness. Self-care, especially as it relates to stress management, was not emphasized by most of our parents or their parents. Our parents, guardians, caretakers, teachers, and others meant no harm but taught us from what they knew. Self-care is not something many of them were skilled in, and it can only be taught to others from a place of self-proficiency. In other words, you can only go as deep with someone else as you are willing to go within yourself. It is as if we have been walking around asleep regarding its importance and doing things that are the opposite of self-care by participating in self-destructive habits.

Some of us have received mixed messages regarding self-care through words or indirect expression that have made caring for one's self to seem selfish, inconsiderate of others, egocentric, narcissistic, etc. We have received the message to put others before ourselves, as if we are not as important. Many people have been shamed as children for not taking better care of their siblings, teammates, friends, and even their parents. For many people, doing things for themselves brings up feelings of guilt as if they should be doing something for someone else instead.

When someone comes to me for assistance, I often start with muscle testing clients regarding their beliefs about caring for themselves. Muscle testing is used in energy medicine to determine subconscious beliefs based on the notion that the body does not lie. When asking the body a question and if the answer is yes or true, the

2   Charles R. Figley, "Compassion Fatigue: An Expert Interview with Charles R. Figley, MS, PhD," interview by Medscape staffer, Medscape.com, October 17, 2005, accessed April 15, 2014, https://www.medscape.com/viewarticle/513615.

muscle tested (usually the arm) will remain strong. If the answer is no or not true, the muscle will go weak. While it seems obvious to many on the conscious level that it is okay to take care of one's self, most do not believe it on a subconscious level. We often begin our work with repatterning subconscious beliefs to be affirmative and congruent with the following statements:

- It is okay for me to take care of myself.
- It's okay for me to honor myself and my needs.
- I am committed to my self-care and make it a priority each day.
- I take responsibility for myself and allow others to take responsibility for themselves.
- I matter.

Although my clientele consists of highly functioning and productive people in service, most do not pass the muscle tests regarding the affirmations above. Our society has considered selfless service to be ideal when what we really need is service from the full use of self. Following the subconscious-belief repatterning work, clients report feeling positive about caring for themselves, which makes it easier to make positive changes and engage in self-care practices. It is a good starting point as doing deeper inner work requires a strong base. Self-care is the best foundation I know for building the stability required for diving deep within held emotions, beliefs, and traumas.

In 2012, as a practicum student, I designed and facilitated a five-week educational series for a women's shelter staff, which consisted mostly of social workers. The series included information regarding nutrition, mindfulness meditation, and stress-relief methods. During the first session, I did a subconscious-belief repatterning exercise with each participant regarding being okay with taking care of one's self. None of them passed the muscle test initially, so the work was essential. It was amazing to watch the transformation of the staff! Many posted their new affirmation within their workspaces. ("It is okay for me to take care of myself.") They went from getting fast food each day to bringing healthy lunches to work. They began taking lunch breaks and often left to walk outside or engage in something rejuvenating. They started participating in activities to help relieve their stress—anything from meditation to kickboxing. They began sharing which self-care techniques were working for them during staff meetings. They became more positive within themselves, and this was noticeable within the organization and the service they provided.

If you struggle with beginning or maintaining a self-care practice, I encourage you to consider subconscious-belief repatterning or some effective form of therapy to get personal blocks out of the way. If you have a positive mind frame around self-care, it will seem natural and enjoyable rather than yet another thing to do.

Create Space for Self-Care

> *Between stimulus and response there is a space. In that space is our power to choose our response. In our response lies our growth and our freedom.*
> **—Viktor Frankl,**
> Austrian neurologist and psychiatrist (Goodreads.com)

One of the first objections people have regarding self-care is that they do not have enough time. Many say they have not enough time for everything on their plates and put themselves last, which often means they get nothing in the end. There are only 24 hours in a day and 365 days in a year. Nothing is going to change that, so it is imperative that we look at ourselves and our lives and make space for what we want to create. This means letting go of the things that do not serve or are of low priority.

I encourage you to be very mindful of the activities you engage in and the habits/patterns you repeat. Taking an honest look at which aspects of life are beneficial and which aspects are outdated or counterproductive can help you decide what to continue with and what needs to go. We often engage in activities and habits that do not serve us out of habit and lack of awareness. As the saying goes, "If you do what you've always done, you'll get what you always got." Putting intention and consciousness behind everything you do will yield powerful results.

A good place to start is by looking at how you spend your time. What are the activities that you fill your schedule with? You might evaluate why you spend your precious moments this way and whether it truly benefits you. For example, people are spending more time on their technology by engaging in social media, playing games on their phones, constantly checking emails and text messages. Many people are attached to these devices to the point where they have become addicted. In my practice, I have found that nearly 20 percent of my clients say technology is one of the major sources of their stress. It can decrease our focus by creating multiple interruptions throughout the day. People can get sucked into the drama on social media, which can get rather nasty.

Speaking of media, many people report feeling stress following watching the news. Is that any surprise, as most of the news reported is focused on the negative things happening? This negativity can create fear in the viewer and keeps people from focusing on what is happening in their present lives. For those who are empathic, watching the news could be even more negatively impactful.

According to Judith Orloff, MD, *empaths* are "people who are highly attuned to other people's emotions." They have the ability to feel and sense the energy of people and the environment around them. They can take on negativity, such as anger or anxiety, which can be exhausting. Many people are unaware that they are empaths, which can make personal energy management confusing and difficult.[3] I will spend some time on it in chapter 9.

Pay attention to how you are affected by your habits around the usage of technology, watching the news and television shows, and the information you expose yourself to. Everything has energy. According

---

[3]   Judith Orloff, *The Empath's Survival Guide* (Boulder, Colorado: Sounds True, 2017), 1–27.

to famous theoretical physicist Albert Einstein, "Everything is energy and that's all there is to it. Match the frequency of the reality you want and you cannot help but to get that reality. It can be done no other way. This is not philosophy. This is physics."[4] Everything has as an energetic frequency, including our thoughts and emotions, and we can attune to the vibrations in the world around us. Consider the frequencies you desire to align with. Do you want to carry the energy of the drama on reality TV, the negativity of the news, etc.?

Research has become focused on how epigenetics affects our gene expression, so it is wise to use awareness with what you are exposing yourself to. According to an article in *Psychology Today*, "It used to be thought that we were born with a fixed genetic blueprint that determined our traits, behaviors, and health. Now, discoveries in the field of epigenetics have radically rebooted this theory by demonstrating that our DNA is more of a switchboard than a blueprint. Epigenetics is the study of how external forces, such as your environment and life experiences, trigger on-off mechanisms on the genetic switchboard. Epigenetic scientists are examining the mechanisms by which genes become expressed or silenced with the goal of understanding how we can influence their activity and change our genetic health outcomes."[5]

The good news here is, you get to create the reality you desire. If you do not like the way things are going, you have the power to change them. You can decide what you engage in and what to turn away from. You can set boundaries around your time and activities. If you do not like the way you feel during or after you watch the news, you can change your habits around it. You may choose to read the news in the newspaper or online if that is more tolerable. You might choose to watch it less often, just enough to have some awareness regarding the bigger stories. You can choose not to watch it at all. You may desire to disengage from social media if you find it takes up too much time, focus, and energy. You might decide to set boundaries

4   Albert Einstein, "Everything Is Energy," quote, Quote Investigator.com, accessed July 8, 2019. https://quoteinvestigator.com/2012/05/16/everything-energy/.
5   "Epigenetics," *Psychology Today*, June 24, 2014, https://www.psychologytoday.com/us/basics/epigenetics/.

around your phone usage and settings. For example, you can turn off push notifications and designate a certain time frame each night in which you check your phone for text, voice, and email messages.

If the activities you engage in are creating chaos and stress in your life, you can change this very easily by simplifying. By reducing time spent on such pursuits, setting boundaries around them, or disengaging from them, you will find time to do other things that are more relaxing and rejuvenating. You may choose to set designated times to unplug. For example, this can be done by taking the weekend to do a digital detox by completely disengaging from your devices. This means turning and keeping the phone, your computer, and other electronics off. It is advisable to let loved ones and those who are in your inner circle know of your plans, so they are not concerned when they cannot reach you.

You can choose to be in the world but not of the world. If it does not resonate with you and what you desire to create in your life, you do not have to do it or you can do less of it. Mindful living involves the use of awareness to create the reality we desire rather than blindly accepting and adopting the latest trend or doing what everyone else is doing.

> *Everything changes*
> *when you start to emit your own*
> *frequency rather than absorbing*
> *the frequencies around you, when*
> *you start imprinting your intent on*
> *the Universe rather than receiving*
> *an imprint from existence.*
> **—Barbara Marciniak,**
> author (Goodreads.com)

I live a simple life that is rather spacious and have chosen not to watch the news, not to engage in social media until it becomes important for my career, not to watch television and have set boundaries around my technology usage. In my world, there is no need to

SUZIE DEVAUGHN

have my phone ringer on all the time or to carry it around everywhere I go. Emails only get checked a few times a day, and when I am
busy or do not feel like talking, the phone is turned off and people
can leave a message. I decide how my time is spent, not the people
and world around me. This leaves time to enjoy my family, exercise,
meditate, cuddle with my dog, and take relaxing baths daily. It creates space and openings for self-care throughout the day. It allows me
to feel grounded and centered in my life, filled with inspiration and
creativity, and energized throughout the day. As a result, it is easier to
be present with my children, enjoy offering services to others without
feeling drained, and truly live life from moment to moment.

We can do cleaning from the outside-in by clearing our space,
including our home and office spaces. Organizing and getting rid of
things you no longer need, use, or love can leave a space feeling open,
bright, and free. Most people report feeling lighter and more efficient
after doing deep cleaning or getting rid of things they no longer need
or that no longer serve them. It may be that positive feeling of accom-
plishment when such endeavors have been completed or the feeling
of freedom from letting go. Additionally, it feels great to donate those
things we no longer want to someone who is in need. It can take
some motivation to get started on cleaning, clearing, and organizing
projects, but the benefits are well worth it. You may even be able to
find additional space for you to meditate, exercise, or engage in creative projects. Some questions I encourage you to ask yourself when
going through your space are the following:

- Do I need this?
- When is the last time I used this?
- Does this still serve me?
- Do I love this?

Answering these questions may help you get the answer you
need regarding whether to hold on or release something. If you are
still having difficulty, imagine what it would feel like to see someone
who just happily found your item at a second-hand store. For example, picture a person who is thrilled that she just found your sweater,

a real treasure. It may give you peace to know that someone will be wearing it soon rather than to leave it folded up on a shelf in your closet for another couple of years without use.

Sometimes we hang on to things because we do not like the discomfort or pain experienced as we release them. Letting go of things, especially those that have an emotional attachment, can be like plucking roots out of your core. This can be especially true with gifts, love letters, cards, items that remind you of past times whether pleasant or difficult. Regardless, these all have energy and can lighten up a space when they are discarded. They can also help liberate you on the inside.

I would like to share a personal example that was very impactful. During the holiday break prior to graduation from graduate school, I took time to do some deep cleaning and clearing. I was already fairly organized and had a place for everything. At least yearly, I would clean and organize all the closets, drawers, cabinets, and garage. This time I decided to go deeper and went through every square inch of my house looking for anything that I did not like, did not need, did not serve me, or had a connection to the past. I was ready for a new beginning and knew that the past must be fully released to create the life I desired. Old cards, love letters, clothes, wedding gifts, music CDs, memorabilia (examples include letter jacket, cheerleading uniform), and the list goes on had to go.

I was like a hurricane tearing through the house for six days, getting rid of massive amounts of stuff. The next four days were spent doing the same thing in the garage, a place that was foreign and a little scary to me. I figured why keep these tools if I do not know how to use them. In the letting go, there was a lot of discomfort, but my desire to be lighter and freer overrode my desire to hang on to them.

When the cleaning project was completed, I opened the windows, did a smudging ritual to release the energy stirred up in my home and to further lighten my space. I had an appointment with my chiropractor/kinesiologist following the project. Without saying a word of my recent accomplishments, he inquired about my activities because it seemed like I had been plucking roots out of my core. I told him about my cleaning project, and he indicated that there would be another purge soon. The following day, I left class feeling ill and threw up before leaving the building. I felt amazing afterward, hence the purge, and was permanently changed after this experience, feeling lighter and freer in every way, including the loss of eight pounds. The irony is, many of the clothes donated would have fit again minus the eight pounds I released. No regrets, there was something about all of it that had to go, and had I held on, perhaps the weight would have remained.

We can also affect our external world by creating and clearing space internally. Are there beliefs, emotions, attachments, relation-ships, and/or habits within yourself that you would like to release? Are there activities you still do that are no longer of benefit or people you spend time with that drain your energy or you no longer enjoy? These are questions worth contemplating, and if the answer is yes, now is a good time to release that which no longer serves you to cre-ate more spaciousness.

Perhaps a therapist or life coach could be beneficial. It is possible that starting or improving upon your exercise regimen, bettering your current eating habits, taking up a new hobby, or spending time in nature would be enjoyable. Making more space for yourself to take pause, con-template, and relax could be what you do with the additional space created. We can sometimes feel resentful of the time and effort given to others when we are not spending enough time meeting our own needs. Self-awareness regarding personal requirements and responding to them can help us restore balance and peace within a busy life.

I invite you to think on these things as you read the book and put intentions into what you want to keep, let go of, and bring into your life. It is helpful to evaluate that which is working well and that which is no longer working in your life. Contemplate how you can make space and take action. By doing so, you are sure to find some time in your schedule for yourself and your self-care. Here are some things to contemplate pertaining to letting go:

- I am ready or need to release these physical things...
- These beliefs I have about myself and/or the world do not serve me...

- I would like to change these patterns of behavior, thinking, actions…
- I want to release these grudges…
- I need to heal the pain around these people, events, traumas, etc. from the past…
- This person/these people are not good for me…
- My addictions include…
- I am overly attached to…
- I am ready to let go of…
- I plan to do this by…
- I want _____ in my life…

Self-Care Toolbox

As you continue reading, I encourage you to consider creating or adding to your self-care toolbox. A kit of ideas and qualified people to assist with self-care is helpful to draw upon to keep one's self replenished. Using self-awareness to continually monitor personal needs and energy level is essential for optimal self-care. Different situations call for different tools and having several to choose from, depending on the circumstance, is beneficial. I recommend doing something to nurture and relax yourself daily. It is even better if you can do several things for yourself throughout the day. Doing so can help you maintain balance and resiliency during times of stress.

Your toolbox can include anything positive you do for yourself that helps to relieve stress, nurtures you and/or revitalizes your energy. Only you know what works best for you. Seeking out new tools to add to those you already use can be invigorating and fun. Example of self-care tools include meditation, breath work, sea/Epsom salt baths, nature walks, exercise, journaling, tapping (Emotional Freedom Technique), Reiki, and acupressure-point massage.

It is also recommended to have a team of qualified professionals whom you can call upon to assist with your self-care needs. Examples include a counselor/therapist, life coach, exercise trainer, massage therapist, chiropractor, acupuncturist. Appointments with trained and knowledgeable professionals can be scheduled regularly as maintenance (a monthly massage, for example) or scheduled as needed.

Support from trusted friends, peers, mentors, and/or supervisors is an important part of a self-care toolbox. The people who you work with can be a great resource because they can closely identify with work stressors and situations encountered.

Identifying, building, and utilizing your self-care toolbox is a great way to create the resiliency necessary to handle the stress of daily living. By taking care of your needs, you will have more energy to give others including your family, friends, clients, patients, and the rest. It is helpful to brainstorm the three categories mentioned and to write them down, including contact information. Sometimes when we are stressed out, it is difficult to know what we most need. Having a list ready with ideas can get you started during those times.

Self-Care I Do for Myself

Examples
- Breath work
- Meditate
- Walk outside
- Yoga class
- Yoga/stretching at home
- Jump on rebounder
- Listen to nature sounds
- Take sea salt bath with candles
- Massage acupressure points
- Journaling

Professionals Who Assist with My Self-Care

	Name	Number
Examples		
• Light tissue massage/ energy work	_____	_____
• Deep-tissue massage	_____	_____

- Rolfing / myofascial release   _____   _____
- Therapy   _____   _____
- Reiki   _____   _____
- Pedicure   _____   _____
- Float tank   _____   _____
- Chiropractor/kinesiologist   _____   _____
- Acupuncture   _____   _____

Social Supports to Assist with My Self-Care

Examples
- Dinner with best friend
- Call sister-in-law
- Lunch with mentor
- Meet with boss
- Girls' night out
- Meditation group
- Date night with partner
- Special one-on-one time with kids

Balance

The key to keeping your balance is knowing when you've lost it.
—Anonymous,
Optimizeme.com

There is a balance to everything, and as you focus on your self-care practice, you are likely to lead a more stable life. It is important to have awareness regarding where you feel balanced within your life and where you do not. With awareness and focus, you can correct the imbalances. For example, there is an equilibrium between doing for others and for yourself, between doing and being, between time spent alone and with others, between masculine and feminine energies, between professional and personal life, between working and recreational activities.

Many people report feeling off-balance as it pertains to their work and personal lives. This can include working long hours, working through lunch, continuously thinking about work while at home, and so on. Prolonged exposure to stress with intensity, duration, and persistence can lead to burnout. Burnout can lead to loss of idealism, energy, motivation, low self-esteem, poor attitude, and reduced effectiveness. A sign of burnout is no longer finding enjoyment in a job that was once enjoyable. When this happens, the remedy often includes making a change. The ideal is to get and stay in balance to avoid experiencing burnout.

We can even get out of equilibrium while doing things we enjoy and have immense passion for. When I first began Self-Care Specialists, I was so excited that every moment free of my children was spent creating and working. Within a few months, fatigue set in, and I realized there was not enough mindless fun and entertainment into my life. Boundaries had to be set around my time, and the computer was shut off five o'clock each night to get a break from my labor of love. By doing so, I regained my balance and felt more invigorated by my work again.

The first step to regaining balance is recognizing that you are out of balance and how. Then you can set boundaries around your time and begin doing things that you have been missing in your life. Balance is something that is fluid, so it is important to pay attention. You may have great balance at one time and then really struggle with it at other times. When you start to notice feeling you have lost your equilibrium, it is important to swing things the other way before it becomes a problem.

I would like to spend some time addressing other areas of balance that are important to maintain self-care practices. One that is most obvious, yet a struggle, is balancing doing things for others and doing things for one's self. Many of us are in service, helping others through our professions. Then we come home and tend to significant others, the children, grandchildren, pets, and others. Too much time spend on helping others can leave us feeling depleted, taken for granted, and resentful. It is important to carve out opportunities to do what you need and enjoy. Sometimes we have to say "later" or "no" to others to say "yes" to ourselves. It is encouraged to set boundaries and speak with your loved ones about what you are feeling and need. It may be uncomfortable as you train yourself and those around you to honor your requirements, but I assure you that everyone will benefit in the long term. You will be more present, less stressed, and more enjoyable.

Sometimes the issue is around over giving and not being open to receive from others. People often have blockages around being open to receive, which can impede financial abundance, affection from others, help from others, appreciation from others, and more. These blockages can often stem from deep feelings of undeserving and unworthiness.

It is important to have the ability to balance doing and being. I consider *doing* to be partaking in getting things done or business-doing activities. This can include working, errands, housework, yard work, exercising, and socializing. I consider *being* to be engaging in interests that involve stillness. Examples include sitting quietly on the deck, resting on the couch (without television), taking a quiet bath, meditating, and other peaceful activities. It is interesting that we are called *human beings*, yet in the Western culture, there are many who struggle with slowing down enough to enjoy being. To be truly balanced, it involves the ability to do both. If you observe yourself feeling uncomfortable with *being*, this may be an area to explore and gain awareness regarding why.

A balance between engaging with one's self and with others is also essential. Why, because there are times when we must do both, and the ability to swing both ways is helpful. Many people tend to be either more introverted or extroverted. You are always with yourself, so having the capacity to enjoy being in your own company is key. The world is full of people, and living in this world involves interacting with them, so comfort in doing so makes life easier on you. It is the things we most struggle with that are our greatest growth opportunities. Whether you get anxious being around others or spending time alone, I assure you the blockage is within yourself and is worth working on clearing. By doing so, you will have more ease within yourself and enjoy living with less restrictions.

Having balance with the areas mentioned above are important for maintaining effective self-care. For example, if you always must be doing something, you may not be giving your body enough rest for rejuvenation and repair. If you do not like spending time alone, you may not create enough space to enjoy quiet introspective moments. If you are always working, whether at the office or around the house, there is not enough time to relax and enjoy life.

Flow

Flow is another aspect that is important to self-care. Everything has a natural rhythm, and when we go with the flow, things seem to go better than when we push against it. This holds true for yourself when you listen to the signals of your body. If you pay attention, it will signal you when it is time to take a break, when it needs movement, nourishment, and so on. For example, there may be certain times of the day when exercise feels natural for you. If you are not a morning person, it might be best to exercise later in the day. Another example, when you are at work and you start feeling tension in your shoulders, it might be time to take a short break to stretch or walk down the hall. Sometimes we push through what we are doing without paying attention when taking a few minutes to address the need would prevent further tension.

It is also helpful to flex and flow with how you feel in each moment and with the windows of time that open in the moment. Chances are that if you do what you feel led to do in a moment, you will be more productive and enjoy what you are doing more. Sometimes this requires giving yourself permission to change plans. For instance, today I had planned to write all day. Upon waking, I felt like running errands, which is not usually appealing to me. The errands were happily run early, and upon returning home, I spent an hour and a half writing. I began to feel the urge to move my body.

It is snowing, so a walk is out. I cleaned the house for a few hours; another chore that is not appealing. My needs to get out of the house in the morning and to move my body were satisfied, and then the urge to sit down and write some more set in. Perhaps I will not write as much as I had planned, but I got several things off my to-do list quickly and joyfully. Windows of time to write more later in the week have been created since the errands and cleaning are out of the way. Additionally, I will have time for a long yoga class tomorrow morning.

The external world also seems to have a flow of its own. Like a river that flows, sometimes rapid and turbulent and sometimes slow and gentle. It also seems to change directions at a moment's notice. We often think we do not have enough time, but sometimes the Universe provides windows of time we are not expecting. For example, when a client reschedules, a meeting gets canceled, or your child gets invited to a sleepover. these can be opportunities to do some self-care. It is encouraged to have some degree of preparedness for when things like this come up. For example, I keep walking shoes, a yoga mat, and workout clothes in my car. If I get to one of my kids' sports practices before it is over, it is an opportunity to go out and walk on the track until he/she is done. If a client texts that he/she needs to reschedule, I may stop by the yoga studio to enjoy a class before resuming my day. If a client is running behind, it is a good time to do a few minutes of breath work.

I like to use the metaphor of a surfer waiting for the perfect wave. The surfer hangs out waiting for the perfect wave, and when it appears, he/she hops on the board and surfs. I don't sit around waiting for windows of time, but if the intention is set to get a workout in today—even if it's a busy day—I will take the opportunity when a window of time presents itself. Our schedules can tend to have some fluidity, and being able to take advantage of the changes that occur rather than getting irritated with them can be advantageous.

On the other hand, it is helpful to schedule self-care into your day and to have routines that meet your self-care needs. For example, getting up early enough for a healthy breakfast, taking time away from the office to eat lunch, getting exercise in after work, and meditating or taking a sea salt bath before bed to unwind. I like to think of those as the givens and the windows of time that show up as icing on the cake.

Ego-Resiliency Scale

Throughout this book, you will have the opportunity to take self-assessments to get in touch with yourself, your ways of thinking, behaviors, reactions, and habits. The ego-resiliency scale assesses *psychological resilience*, defined as "the capacity of the individual to effectively modulate an ever-changing complex of desires and reality constraints."[6] Ego-resiliency can be positively impacted and changed by implementing and practicing effective self-care. The Ego-Resiliency Scale is included here to learn more about your characteristics and how you handle certain situations. This scale and its description were obtained, with permission to use, from Figley Institute's *Counterbalance the Intensity of Your Work: Compassion Stress Management Workbook.* Developer of the scale is in the footnotes.

---

[6] J. Block, and A. M. Kremen, "IQ and Ego-Resiliency: Conceptual and Empirical Connections and Separateness," *Journal of Personality Social Psychology* 70, no. 2 (1996): 349–361.

Ego-Resiliency Scale[7]

The Ego-Resiliency Scale consists of fourteen items, each with a corresponding four-point Likert scale, ranging from 1 (does not apply at all) to 4 (applies very strongly). Record the score for each of the items, giving you fourteen scores, and add the scores and check out the "Scoring Interpretation."

Statements	(1) Does not apply at all	(2) Applies slightly	(3) Applies some-what	(4) Applies very strongly
1. I am generous with my friends.	1	2	3	4
2. I quickly get over and recover from being startled.	1	2	3	4
3. I enjoy dealing with new and unusual situations.	1	2	3	4
4. I usually succeed in making a favorable impression on people.	1	2	3	4
5. I enjoy trying new foods I have never tasted before.	1	2	3	4
6. I am regarded as a very energetic person.	1	2	3	4

---

7   J. Block, and A. M. Kremen, "IQ and Ego-Resiliency: Conceptual and Empirical Connections and Separateness," *Journal of Personality Social Psychology* 70, no. 2 (1996): 349–361.

7. I like to take different paths to familiar places.	1	2	3	4
8. I am more curious than most people.	1	2	3	4
9. Most of the people I meet are likable.	1	2	3	4
10. I usually think carefully about something before acting.	1	2	3	4
11. I like to do new and different things.	1	2	3	4
12. My daily life is full of things that keep me interested.	1	2	3	4
13. I would be willing to describe myself as a pretty *strong* personality.	1	2	3	4
14. I get over my anger at someone reasonably quickly.	1	2	3	4

Scoring Interpretation

Score	47–56	35–46	23–34	11–22	0–10
Trait Level	Very High Resiliency Trait	High Resiliency Trait	Undetermined Trait	Low Resiliency Trait	Very Low Resiliency Trait

Summary

Self-care is anything that you do to take care of your well-being. It is beneficial to lay a foundation from which your self-care practices can further evolve. An important component to carrying out effective self-care is how you feel both consciously and subconsciously about taking care of your needs. If there are any beliefs or feelings that keep you from feeling good about taking care of yourself, you will want to transform these to become positive to prevent self-sabotage. Creating space for yourself and your self-care is essential, or there will not be time to take care of your needs. You'll want to identify many tools to keep in your self-care toolbox such as things you do for yourself, professionals who assist with your wellness, and other people who support you in meeting your personal care goals. Using mindfulness to assess your balance at any given time is useful. The best way to get back to balance is realizing when you have lost it.

CHAPTER 3

Physical Self-Care

Our bodies are our gardens to which our wills are our gardeners.
—William Shakespeare,
Quora.com

The physical aspects of self-care are what most people think of when they envision wellness and taking care of one's self. This dimension of self-care is the foundation for healthy living. The body is the temple for the mind, spirit, and soul and must be cared for to maintain life. We can go far beyond meeting the body's basic needs for survival by taking our physical self-care to a new level. For example, eating food will meet the body's need for fuel. We can survive on food, but we can eat quality food with mindfulness and give the body what it needs to thrive.

In this chapter, I will not get into the science of physical self-care, as there are plenty of research studies that validate what is said. I will be speaking from experience and hope to give you some things to consider for yourself. You are free to choose that which resonates with you and further explore what interests you. Ultimately, you will decide upon the prescription that is optimal for you. Sometimes it is trial and error, but as we connect with the body, it gives us the answers regarding what works for us and that which does not. We are each unique down to our DNA and must learn to listen to and trust our bodies to guide us.

One of the lessons learned on my quest for better health was listening to and trusting my body above all else. I was given prescriptions, advice, and recommendations regarding how to improve my condition, some of which were helpful, but some were not. Initially, I blindly trusted the doctors and gave away my personal power, believing that they must know better because of their education and credentials. I eventually learned that the ultimate guidance came from within. Through connection with my body and intuition (my inner knowing), I was able to sense what to do and not do. My body spoke loudly when the approach did not work with signals such as pain, discomfort, bloating and/or gas. When something resonated with me, it felt as if my body hummed and became energized. It was a slow process of experimentation that eventually got me where I needed to be.

Healthy Diet

The doctor of the future will no longer treat the human frame with drugs, but rather will cure and prevent disease with nutrition.
—Thomas Edison
(Goodreads.com)

The nourishment we provide our bodies is of utmost importance because it creates the energy that fuels our bodies. Let us use the metaphor of a car. If you put the wrong gasoline into a car, it does not run as well, and if you run out of oil, the engine could burn up.

If you use the correct gasoline for the model, get regular oil changes, tire alignments, and do maintenance as necessary, the car will run smoother and longer. The human body is far more complex than a car, but like a car, we do not function as well when we put the wrong food into our bodies. Unfortunately, some people treat their cars better than their bodies.

There are many ways of eating, and there is no one approach that works for everyone. You have the freedom to choose how you eat. I prefer to look at the way we eat as a lifestyle rather than a *diet*. The thing we do have in common is that our bodies need food, which the body converts into energy to be used as fuel to keep it running. Some people are fine with the body running with aches and pings, and some prefer to functional optimally, like a Ferrari on a smoothly paved highway. The second scenario takes more effort and discipline, but the payoff will be demonstrated in the way you feel.

There are so many options available that are convenient for people who are busy and on the go. Fast food, freezer meals, and canned food are readily available but do not have the same nutritional density as fresh, natural food. Eating foods that are free of pesticides, added hormones, steroids, preservatives, and food colorings is best for the body. These foods are becoming more accessible through health food stores, natural foods sections in grocery stores, and even fast-food chains are changing their menus. Fortunately, things are evolving, and natural foods are becoming mainstream. We are realizing a need to get back to the dietary basics, the way our ancestors and earlier civilizations ate.

With so many diets to choose from, people often struggle with where to get started. Regardless of the edibles chosen, it is helpful to incorporate the standard of natural food (free of pesticides, herbicides, added hormones, steroids, preservatives, and food colorings). Otherwise, explore and choose a dietary regimen that resonates with your body and helps you to reach your goals (which could include energy optimization, weight loss, weight gain, etc.)

Here Is Some Simple Advice

Eat less crap.
    C—carbonated drinks
    R—refined sugar
    A—artificial sweeteners and colors
    P—processed foods
Eat more food.
    F—fruits and vegetables
    O—organic lean proteins
    O—omega-3 fatty acids
    D—drink water[8]

Simple Definitions of Dietary Lifestyle Choices

Atkins Diet: Dr. Atkins, a well-known cardiologist, recommends a diet which limits sugar and carbohydrates, so the body burns fat as fuel. This approach leaves the body steadily fueled; weight is lost even when more calories are being consumed. Steady fueling also means more constant energy levels all day, less hunger, and cravings.[9]

Blood-Type Diet: This diet recommends types of foods to eat and avoid based on the person's blood type—O, A, B, or AB. Created by D'Adamo, a naturopath, the diet claims that the foods you eat react chemically with your blood type. If you follow a diet designed for your blood type, you will digest food more efficiently, you will lose weight, have more energy, and it helps prevent disease.[10]

Gluten-Free Diet: This diet excludes the protein gluten found in grains such as wheat, barley, rye, and a cross between wheat and rye called triticale. A gluten-free diet is essential in managing signs

---

[8]   Peggy Malone, "Eat Less Crap, Eat More Food," Dr.PeggyMalone.com, October 10, 2013, accessed July 25, 2020, https://drpeggymalone.com/eat-crap-eat-food/.

[9]   "How a Low Carb Diet Works?" How It Works, Atkins, accessed June 24, 2019. https://www.atkins.com/how-it-works.

[10] Stephanie Watson, "The Blood Type Diet,". WebMD, accessed June 24, 2019. https://www.webmd.com/diet/a-z/blood-type-diet.

and symptoms of celiac disease and other medical conditions associated with gluten. This diet has become popular among people without gluten-related medical conditions due to the claimed benefits of improved digestion, weight loss, increased energy, and better overall health.[11]

Glycemic-Index Diet: The glycemic-index diet is an eating plan based on how foods affect your blood-sugar level. The glycemic index is a system of assigning numbers to carbohydrate-containing foods according to how much each food increases blood sugar. The glycemic index is not a diet plan but a tool for guiding food choices that aids in maintaining healthy blood-sugar levels.[12]

Ketogenic Diet: Used as a popular weight-loss strategy based on eating low carbohydrate so the body goes into *ketosis*, "a normal metabolic process in which fat is burned for energy instead of carbohydrates, which produces ketones." If you are healthy and eating a balanced diet, your body controls how much fat it burns, and you do not normally make or use ketones. But when you cut way back on calories or carbohydrates, the body will switch to ketosis for energy. In addition to helping you burn fat, ketosis can make you feel less hungry and help maintain muscle.[13] Some people swear by this diet, but I highly recommend researching it yourself and seeking medical advice. Studies have shown it to be helpful with some medical conditions, but that it can have some negative side effects.

Mediterranean Diet: It includes eating primarily plant-based foods such as fruits and vegetables, whole grains, legumes, and nuts. Butter is replaced with healthy fats such as olive oil. Herbs and spices are used to flavor foods instead of salt. Red meat is limited to a few times a month. An occasional glass of red wine is acceptable. This

[11] Mayo Clinic Staff, "Gluten-Free Diet," Mayo Clinic, accessed June 24, 2019, https://www.mayoclinic.org/healthy-lifestyle/nutrition-and-healthy-eating/in-depth/gluten-free-diet/art-20048530.

[12] Mayo Clinic Staff, "Glycemic Index Diet: What's Behind the Claims," Mayo Clinic, accessed June 24, 2019, https://www.mayoclinic.org/healthy-lifestyle/nutrition-and-healthy-eating/in-depth/glycemic-index-diet/art-20048478.

[13] WebMD Staff, "What's a Ketogenic Diet?" WebMD, accessed June24 2019, https://www.webmd.com/diet/ss/slideshow-ketogenic-diet.

diet is characterized by the traditional cooking style of countries bordering the Mediterranean Sea. Research has shown this diet can reduce the risk of heart disease by lowering LDL cholesterol. This diet is also associated with reduced occurrence of cancer, breast cancer, Parkinson's, and Alzheimer's diseases.[14]

Paleo Diet: The paleo diet is a dietary plan based on eating foods that are similar to what might have been eaten during the Paleolithic era, which dates from approximately 2.5 million to 10,000 years ago. The diet includes lean meats, fish, vegetables, fruits, nuts, and seeds—foods that were obtained in the past through hunting and gathering. It limits foods that came when farming emerged—such as dairy, legumes, and grains. Benefits reported include weight loss, improved glucose tolerance, improved blood pressure, lower triglycerides, and better appetite management.[15]

Vegan Diet: A vegan diet is free of animal products; it excludes animal protein and fish, is free of dairy and other food products derived from animals. Vegans favor a diet rich in whole foods such as fruits, vegetables, whole grains, legumes, nuts, and seeds. Most vegans require a B-12 supplement, an iron supplement and finding other sources of non-animal protein, such as protein powder.

Vegetarian Diet: A vegetarian diet is like a vegan diet rich in whole foods including fruits, vegetables, whole grains, legumes, nuts, and seeds. There are different types of vegetarian diets. Some include eggs, dairy products, and fish. According to an article in Medical News Today, a vegetarian diet has been found to reduce the risk of heart disease, obesity, hypertension, type 2 diabetes, and some types of cancer. It may also lead to weight loss and a longer life expectancy.

The Zone Diet: It's a diet lifestyle created by Barry Sears, PhD, that includes drinking water before meals; eating a combination of 40 percent low-glycemic carbohydrates of mostly fruits and vege-

---

[14] Mayo Clinic Staff, "Healthy Lifestyle, Nutrition, and Healthy Eating," Mayo Clinic, June 24, 2019, https://www.mayoclinic.org/healthy-lifestyle/nutrition-and-healthy-eating/in-depth/mediterranean-diet/art-20047.

[15] Mayo Clinic Staff, "Paleo Diet: What Is It, and Why Is It so Popular?" Mayo Clinic, accessed June 24, 2019, https://www.mayoclinic.org/healthy-lifestyle/nutrition-and-healthy-eating/in-depth/paleo-diet/art-20111182.

tables, 30 percent lean protein, 30 percent good fats in three meals plus two snacks per day to create a hormonal equilibrium to help you think better, perform better, balance blood sugar, never go hungry, and have more energy.[16]

Superfoods: Eating a diet high in superfoods is recommended. These foods are considered to be some of the most nutritionally dense and have various health benefits. Certain superfoods are so powerful they can be considered medicinal in nature. I will not go into the nutrients included in each food or the benefits; however, if you are curious, it would be worth exploring.[17]

- Dark leafy greens—kale, spinach, lettuce, arugula, swiss chard, collard greens, turnip greens
- Berries—raspberries, strawberries, blueberries, blackberries
- Green tea
- Eggs
- Legumes
- Nuts and seeds—almonds, pistachios, walnuts, cashews, Brazil nuts, macadamia nuts, peanuts, sunflower seeds, pumpkin seeds, chia seeds, flaxseeds, hemp seeds.
- Kefir
- Garlic
- Olive oil
- Ginger
- Turmeric
- Salmon
- Avocado
- Sweet potato
- Mushroom
- Seaweed

---

[16] Barry Sears and, William Lawren, *Mastering the Zone* (New York: HarperCollins, 1997), 25–31.

[17] Ansley Hill, "16 Superfoods That Are Worthy of the Title," Healthline, July 9, 2018, accessed June 24, 2019. https://www.healthline.com/nutrition/true-superfoods.

"Dirty Dozen" Foods: These foods are found to have highest concentration of pesticides by the Environmental Working Group.[18] Thus, it is best to eat these grown organically.

- Strawberries
- Spinach
- Kale
- Nectarines
- Apples
- Grapes
- Peaches
- Cherries
- Pears
- Tomatoes
- Celery
- Potatoes

"Clean Fifteen" Foods: These foods are found to have the lowest concentration of pesticides by the Environmental Working Group. [19]

- Avocados
- Sweet corn
- Pineapple
- Onions
- Papaya
- Sweet peas (frozen)
- Eggplants
- Asparagus
- Cauliflower

---

[18] Environmental Working Group (EWG) Science Team, "EWG's Dirty Dozen for 2020," in EWG's 2020 Shopper's Guide to Pesticides in Produce, March 25, 2020. https://www.ewg.org/foodnews/summary.php.

[19] 20. Environmental Working Group (EWG) Science Team, "EWG's Clean Fifteen for 2020," in EWG's 2020 Shopper's Guide to Pesticides in Produce, March 25, 2020. https://www.ewg.org/foodnews/summary.php.

- Cantaloupes
- Broccoli
- Mushrooms
- Cabbage
- Honeydew melon
- Kiwi

Water

A nutrient that is essential to the body is water. The human body is made up of 70 percent water and must continually be replenished. Drinking filtered water is best. A good rule of thumb is to take your weight, divide it into two and drink at least that many ounces per day of water. There is no substitute for water. Coffee and caffeinated drinks such as pop act as diuretics and actually cause us to lose water. Fruit juices should be consumed in moderation as they contain sugar. In a healthy diet, water is the beverage of choice. Water also continuously flushes the body, which is helpful with detoxification.

Personally, I had to try several things to get a diet that worked well for me. Finally settling on my version of the Zone, which is also organic, gluten-free, grain-free, dairy-free, and very low in sugar. I became vegetarian for five months and felt amazing at first, as my body was loving all the vegetables. Over time, there were signs of protein deficiency and felt led to go back to eating animal protein. I have got a lot of muscle mass and have always needed a lot of protein. My blood type is O, which according to the blood-type diet requires a lot of protein. With the Zone, I still get the benefits of lots of vegetables and good fat. When I eat Zone-appropriate meals and snacks, I feel less hungry. My body weight gravitates to its ideal. I also have more energy, sleep better, and have better workouts.

This way of eating has been my friend for many years. If I eat according to the ratios and rules indicated, most of the time, I am able to eat as much as I want and maintain my ideal healthy weight. The underweight period mentioned was during the health crisis, prior to eating according to the Zone. It corrected my weight issue and low blood sugar. Many years later, I veered away from the Zone and gained thirty-five pounds, a lot for a small frame. It was very confusing to me because I ate very healthy foods. The issue was that I was eating gluten-free grains like rice and corn, which are high on the glycemic index, and was not eating foods in the portions recommended by the Zone (30 percent protein, 30 percent good fat, 40 percent low glycemic carbohydrates).

It is of the utmost importance to pay attention to the signals of your body to help guide you toward the correct nutrition for yourself. What works for one does not necessarily mean it will work for another. And there may be times when eating one way works for you, and then as your body changes, you may need to adjust your nourishment. For many, the word *diet* implies a weight-loss program. Rather than focusing on the aspect of body weight, I like to focus on what and how we eat as food that fuels the body to keep us functioning optimally.

Weight loss or weight gain can be a signal that the way one eats is not working well. Healthy eating best serves as a lifestyle and not something done for a short while to meet a goal, such as weight loss. When you find the formula for you, maintaining ideal weight and energy can become natural and the need to focus on weight falls away. When fed the proper nutrition, the body begins to crave it. The desire to feel good overrides the temporary satisfaction of eating foods that are fried, filled with sugar, void of nutrients, and considered unhealthy.

You can decide how far you want to go with your nutrition. For example, some people eat well during the week and then are more lenient over the weekend. Healthy options for going deeper into nutrition include making nutritionally dense smoothies, juicing, supplementing with superfood-concentrated drinks, and beyond. It has been said that we are not able to get as nourishment from our foods today as in previous years because the quality of the soil has been eroding. The addition of herbicides and pesticides is not helping. I encourage you to consider adding some supplementation, such as a multiple vitamin supplement, probiotics, omega-3 fish oil, and vitamin D. Doing research or seeking the advice from a trained professional is recommended to help figure out what you would most benefit from.

I utilize the assistance of a chiropractor/kinesiologist who does muscle testing to get information regarding the supplements my body would most benefit from. Once the nutrition needs are discovered, he then tests to make sure they work well together synergistically. Every six months or so, he rechecks to make sure the combination previously prescribed is still indicated, either because I noticed a change in my body's response to the supplements, or he noticed a change while working on me. Over the years, I have done this with two professionals in the field, and it has been very advantageous and accurate for me.

I would like to share a few examples of how this method of checking for supplements has helped me. Prior to my introduction to chiropractic/kinesiology work, during my first pregnancy, I struggled with the prenatal vitamins prescribed. My obstetrician and I worked together by trying five or six and eventually went back to my multiple vitamin and added a folic acid supplement. The prescription prenatal vitamins each gave me side effects such as constipation and nausea.

I had begun working with a chiropractor/kinesiologist prior to my second pregnancy. He tested for a prenatal vitamin that resonated with my body. I took it to my ob-gyn to make sure he approved, which he did. I felt amazing on this vitamin and was able to continue taking it for a year postnatal throughout the breastfeeding.

During my third pregnancy, my blood work showed that I was anemic and was told it was because there was not much time between the second and third pregnancies. My obstetrician wanted to prescribe an iron supplement. The idea of guessing which one would work for me is not appealing after the vitamin and constipation issues I had with the first pregnancy. My chiropractor/kinesiologist then did some muscle testing and found a liquid ionic iron supplement that resonated with my body. My ob-gyn approved of the prescription and amount. I felt fantastic on this form of iron and never had constipation or side effects. It was a great compliment to the prenatal vitamin he had muscle tested me for.

Healthy Eating Lifestyle Tips

- Go through your cabinets/refrigerator/freezer and discard/ donate any foods that are unhealthy. If you desire to keep a few treats, place them in the back of the cabinet so they are not the first thing you see when reaching for a snack.
- Stock up on nourishing snacks for home and the office. Examples include nuts and seeds, raisins, dried cranberries, fresh fruit, low-sugar energy bars, and low-sugar yogurt.
- Thoroughly wash all fruits and vegetables.
- Keep fresh cut vegetables in the refrigerator at all times. Examples are carrots, celery, red peppers, cucumbers, cherry tomatoes. They can be eaten alone or paired with something healthy such as hummus, guacamole, and almond butter. You are more likely to munch on these if they are readily available.
- Plan your meals in advance each week. Look at the calendar and decide which nights you will need to cook and which days you can bring your lunch to work. Grocery shop accordingly.
- Eat a healthy breakfast each morning. Simple and nutritious choices include smoothies with fruit/veggie combinations and added flax or chia seeds, fresh juices made in the juicer, omelets with vegetables, egg scrambles with veggies, oatmeal, quinoa, low-sugar granola/cereal/yogurt, turkey bacon, turkey or chicken sausage. A combination of low-glycemic carbohydrates, lean protein and good fat is recommended unless you are vegan/vegetarian.
- Double and triple recipes with the intention of having extra. The remainder can be eaten as leftovers for lunch, another dinner, or frozen for later use. This works especially well with soups, stews, and chili.
- Cook during the weekend for the upcoming week.
- Prepare salad fixings during the weekend so they are easy to throw together for a meal during the week. For example, you can chop a lot of lettuce and prepare veggies/proteins

to have various salads for lunch/dinner during the week. These could include taco salad, chicken Caesar salad, oriental chicken salad, kale salad, and garden salad. You do not need a recipe! You need a good salad dressing (homemade or store bought) and the essentials. I am fond of Primal Kitchen salad dressings because they are made with pure ingredients and avocado oil. Simple!

- Do a meal exchange with a friend who cooks healthy too. For example, one week you make extra for your friend and family and bring enough to them; one week they do the same for you.
- Have a list handy of healthy restaurant options that you enjoy for sit-down dining, carry-out, or delivery for times when you do not feel like cooking or are in a hurry. These can include health food stores, salad bars, delis, etc. Forethought is important here as it will help you resist the urge to hit a fast-food drive-through.

Exercise

Those who think they have not time for bodily exercise will sooner or later have to find time for illness.

—Edward Stanley

(Goodreads.com)

The human body is made to move, and movement is essential in staying healthy and balanced. Exercise is an area of self-care that has been emphasized as early as grade school by our society. Although the benefits of exercise have been researched and are well-known, taking the time to do it or having the energy to move are factors that can keep us from engaging in fitness activities regularly or at all. I will not go scientific during this discussion as I prefer to speak on the subject from my perspective.

Exercise is an essential component within a self-care plan. It is foundational and unless it is recommended by a credible medical professional not to exercise for some reason, should be incorporated into regular self-care. How often is up to you. My recommendation is to do something physical nearly every day to keep the muscles active, lymphatic system moving, blood circulating, and to maintain physical fitness. This can be anything from light, gentle stretching to rigorous workouts. Obviously, you will want to listen to your body and honor its needs. If your energy is low, a rigorous workout may not be in order. There have been times in my life where I had the energy to exercise each day and times, like when I experienced adrenal fatigue, that stretching and a walk to the mailbox were all that could be done. Sometimes we think we do not have the energy to exercise but getting out for a walk ends up giving us more energy.

I recommend incorporating exercise that has these components: strength, flexibility, balance, aerobic conditioning, and endurance. Sometimes it is necessary to do a few different types of exercises to ensure that all the bases are covered. Cross-training is always good to include these areas and work different muscles. For example, it would be beneficial for a runner to do yoga a few times a week to balance the aerobic conditioning and endurance with flexibility and balance. Both workouts are valuable for building and maintaining strength. There was a time when I was doing a lot of Pilates but was not doing enough cardiovascular exercise. Adding brisk walking for thirty minutes to an hour on the off days was an excellent way to balance my Pilates workout, which covered all the areas discussed. Now I do something every day that includes the combination of yoga, brisk walking, jumping on the rebounder, and arm-weight repetitions.

Sleep

Getting adequate sleep is an essential part of self-care. Sleep needs can vary by person, but as a good rule of thumb, seven to eight hours is necessary for adults. Many people do not get enough sleep or sleep poorly and accept that is just how it is. If you have difficulty sleeping or the quality of your sleep is poor, I suggest engaging in good sleep-hygiene practices or habits that foster a good night's sleep. Additionally, doing activities during the day that help relieve stress can encourage better sleep overall. Examples include meditation, breath work, exercise, and other tension-relieving activities can be helpful (more on this later).

Sleep-Hygiene Tips

- Limit naps to thirty minutes.
- Slow down an hour or a few hours before going to sleep. Participate in relaxing activities before bed. These include reading, sea salt baths, meditation, breath work, and gentle stretching. I will write in the upcoming chapter about how to do meditation and breath work.
- Unplug from technology one to two hours before bed. Turn off your ringer, put the phone in another room, and disengage from social media.
- Keep the television, laptops, and tablets somewhere other than your bedroom. Allow this to be an environment mainly designed for sleeping.
- Declutter your sleeping space, as everything has energy and clearing it may make it feel more peaceful.
- Set the thermostat to a comfortable temperature before sleeping.
- Make the room as dark as possible prior to sleep. If you need some light to feel comfortable, you might use a low wattage night-light.
- Wear comfortable sleepwear to bed, appropriate for the time of the year.
- Be sure to have adequate blankets available.
- Stop drinking water an hour or more before bedtime if you get up to urinate often.
- Avoid caffeine or alcohol as these have been known to disrupt sleep.

- If you wake during the night, lull yourself back to sleep with breath work. Deep breathing induces the parasympathetic relaxation response. Allow your abdomen to rise on the inhale and fall on the exhale. Sometimes you can hear a sound in your throat that resembles the ocean, which can relax you back to sleep.

If you have sleep issues, despite good sleep hygiene and stress-management techniques or your issues are severe, I propose speaking to a health-care professional. The root of the sleep issues can be physiological or psychological. Sleep and how it affects the body's functioning are too important to ignore. Low-quality sleep is often due to stress or emotional issues that have not been resolved.

I have worked with many people who report that the quality and duration of their sleep improves when they do the emotional work and learn how to manage their stress. Meditation, breath work, exercise, and other tension-relieving activities have been linked to improved sleep. Additionally, several have benefitted from subconscious-belief repatterning work. Sometimes subconscious beliefs around feeling safe or having the ability to sleep need to be transformed. The messages we tell ourselves can become our beliefs, both consciously and subconsciously. Imagine someone who is having a rough patch and cannot sleep. She gets frustrated and tells herself or others, "I cannot sleep," and this becomes her reality.

I have had several clients with trauma history who had difficulty sleeping. We work with healing the trauma through body-centered psychotherapy but also address the subconscious belief. For example, a client who had been sexually abused by the priest at her church from a young age and at age fifty-five, she could not remember ever having a good night's sleep. We did the emotional healing work necessary and repatterned her subconscious beliefs to include "It is safe for me to sleep at night," and "I sleep deeply and peacefully at night." She began sleeping well for the first time in her life.

If you suspect that the issue is physiological, you will want to address this with a medical doctor or holistic equivalent. It is possible that you could get recommended to a sleep specialist who may recommend further investigation.

It is also possible that you are experiencing adrenal fatigue, which can occur when you are exposed to stress over time or have health issues. When the adrenal glands become exhausted and are not able to produce adequate quantities of hormones, primarily cortisol, they become fatigued. Many alternative-health practitioners diagnose and treat this condition.

I have experienced adrenal fatigue several times in my life for various reasons, health- or stress-related. It impacted my ability to get a good night's sleep, and my sleep quality improved dramatically once I began taking an adrenal-support supplement. Recently I began feeling the onset of adrenal fatigue when a series of positive life changes affected my system. The excitement experienced was overwhelming and affected my ability to settle into sleep. It was like being a two-year-old who was overstimulated and not able to get down for a nap or bed at night. My kinesiologist recommended an herbal adrenal-support supplement that resonated with my body well through muscle testing. The quality of my sleep improved immediately and has since been great. Neither he nor I anticipate the need for adrenal support long-term but is very helpful as I am adjusting to positive changes in my life.

Reduce Your Chemical Load

There are many ways in which we overstress our bodies, including the chemical load we place upon them. The human body seems to function best when it is cared for naturally, yet in today's day and age, we often overlook the unnatural products we use and the effects those have on our health. Placing a large chemical burden on the body can reduce the effectiveness of its organs (e.g., liver and kidneys), systems (e.g., nervous, lymphatic, immune), and more, potentially leading to imbalance and health problems.

Examples of the products we use and consume that often have chemicals include pesticides (used in the home and on our foods), cleaning supplies, laundry soaps, fabric softeners, products used on our skin (e.g., soap, shampoo, lotion), perfume/cologne, and air freshener.

There are healthier versions or replacements of the above products that can be substituted. Green pesticide services that use organic products such as peppermint or rosemary oil rather than harsh chemicals to rid your home of spiders and insects are available in some locations. A mixture of white vinegar and water can be utilized as a cleaning solution that has antibacterial and antifungal properties. Green cleaning products are easy to find at health food stores, in grocery stores, and discount stores.

"Free and clear" versions of laundry soap are preferable to those with fragrance and dyes. These and green versions can easily be found where you usually purchase detergent and at health food stores. Eliminating the use of fabric softener or using green versions is the best way to avoid irritation and/or chemical exposure to the skin. Natural soaps and sulfate-free shampoos are best for the skin and can be found in health food stores and natural product sections in most grocery markets. Reducing or eliminating perfumes, colognes, and air fresheners can also help lighten your chemical load. Essential oils can be used as a natural replacement of perfumes and air fresheners.

As previously mentioned, organic food can be purchased which is free of pesticides and herbicides often used in the growth and production process. Meat that is labeled free of antibiotics and steroids is more available than ever. These foods can be purchased at health food stores or in the natural foods section of the grocery store. If you cannot afford to buy organic food or are unsure of where to begin, you can start by avoiding the "dirty dozen" foods (listed on page 59). These are the foods that have been found to have the highest concentration of pesticides and herbicides.

It is important to include methods of detoxification into your self-care regimen. It is recommended that you seek the advice of your medical doctor, holistic doctor, or appropriate health-care professional if you have questions regarding detoxification methods or beginning a new detoxifying regimen. Some gentle methods of detoxification are listed below. If you suspect that you have an issue with excess heavy metals or chemicals in your body, address this with a medical professional. Testing can be done to assess heavy metal burden and chelation therapy is often recommended to bind and pull toxins out of the body.

Gentle Methods of Detoxification

- Eat greens on a regular basis (romaine and dark-leaf lettuce, kale, spinach, broccoli, cabbage, celery, green bell pepper, leeks, cilantro, parsley)
- Add fresh smoothies and juices to your diet (including certain foods known to detoxify the organs such as apples, lemons, greens, ginger, beets, celery, cranberries, cilantro, dandelion leaf)
- Add spirulina, chlorella, sea kelp, and/or wheatgrass to your diet
- Drink plenty of filtered water
- Do medically recommended or supervised cleanses
- Take Essiac tonic when feeling toxic (found in health food stores, follow directions on the label)
- Drink detoxifying teas (ex. lemongrass, ginger, dandelion, milk thistle, nettle leaf, detoxifying herb blends)
- When feeling toxic, use activated charcoal as it binds unwanted materials and gas, then carries it safely through the digestive system (found in health food stores, follow directions on the label)
- Exercise to the point of perspiration several times a week
- Sit in an infrared sauna (no longer than thirty minutes)
- Take regular Epsom or sea salt baths (add one to two cups of salt to a bath as warm as you are comfortable for thirty minutes)

Taking a natural approach to caring for your body is helpful to keep it functioning optimally. Awareness regarding chemical exposure and detoxification methods is important. Fortunately, replacements and substitutions for products containing chemicals are readily available. Going *green* or getting back to nature with your self-care is another great way to ease the stress put upon your body. The added benefit is that it is also great for the people around you and for the planet.

Preventative Checkups, Screens, and Maintenance

It is advisable to include preventative checkups in your self-care strategy. Practitioners may include your family physician, ob-gyn, functional medicine doctor, dentist, eye doctor, chiropractor, acupuncturist, and more. Depending on your general health, special needs, and age, there may be screens that are recommended by your health-care provider such as blood tests, cholesterol check, mammogram, pap smear, skin check, colonoscopy, and others. It is your choice to decide which types of health-care providers to include within your self-care. I personally like to include the best of both Eastern and Western medicine. Your belief system is likely to guide this but consider being open to trying new things if the approaches you have been using are not working well for you.

Summary

Physical self-care including healthy diet and eating habits, regular exercise, adequate quality sleep, awareness regarding chemical load, and detoxification methods are essential for maintaining health and wellness. A nutritious and healthy diet helps the body to have the proper fuel to thrive. The body needs to move, and regular exercise keeps us physically fit and the systems functioning as they were designed to do. The body needs quality sleep for rest and repair. Reducing the body's chemical load and detoxification methods are essential for keeping the body working in optimal condition. Physical self-care is foundational and is a great place to begin a self-care practice. All this takes time and effort, and there are no magic pills or shortcuts, but you are worth the investment. If you commit to your physical care, you are sure to see the results of feeling better, having more energy, looking better, improved performance, and beyond.

CHAPTER 4

Psychological Self-Care

*Peace can be a lens through
which you see the world. Be
it. Live it. Radiate it out.
Peace is an inside job.*
—Wayne Dyer,
Habitswellbeing.com

Stress management and the mental/emotional aspects of self-care are of the utmost importance and often get overlooked. Some wait until everything has gone wrong before seriously considering psychological self-care. Many people neglect this area because they believe they are too busy, and it does take some time. We must live with ourselves each day of our lives, so how we think and feel about the person inside and the world around us is crucial. It not only affects us and our well-being, but it impacts the people around us and the reality that we create for ourselves.

Everyone experiences difficulties and challenges as we live our lives. It is essential to learn how to navigate life's challenges successfully without suffering from ongoing future effects. These challenges are opportunities for growth but can leave us feeling defeated, depleted, and traumatized if they are not handled appropriately. If we do not fully process and resolve difficult situations within us, they can result in the formation of faulty belief systems, sabotaging patterns, held negative emotional energy, and trauma. People often get into trouble when they try to ignore or go around the emotions of difficult situations rather than going through them. As humans, we often do anything to avoid feeling discomfort and pain, yet it is part of the human experience. The greatest healing comes from the ability to feel what you feel, with acceptance and compassion. Doing this work can be difficult and require great vulnerability, but strength can be found by working at great depth. Doing inner work can leave us truly thriving, not just surviving.

It is easy to look at our problems as things that exist outside of us instead of looking within to find what we are responsible for or have created. It is easy to play the blame game and not even realize we are acting like victims instead of using self-awareness to see how our unhealthy patterns of behavior, faulty belief systems, and emotional maneuvering have contributed to or created the situations in our lives. It is an inside job, and the answers we seek usually lie within ourselves. The solutions to our problems can often be solved by going within and working on inner transformation.

The greatest gift we can give to others is to live and work from a place of wholeness found within ourselves. The gifts we receive by doing our inner work can include the ability to connect deeply with self and others, compassion, wisdom, intuition, clarity, and an unwavering inner compass. We have the honor and opportunity to touch the lives of everyone we interact with. It is our responsibility to start with ourselves. Connect deeply with your heart and soul, and everyone will benefit, including yourself.

There are a variety of things you can do for psychological self-care discussed in this chapter, ranging from stress management to doing deep inner work. It is recommended to get a self-care foundation prior to diving into deep inner work. The social readjustment rating scale is included below for reflection regarding stressful situations you may have encountered within the past twelve months. Keep in mind that while many of the events listed are considered positive by most, they can have an effect within the body and mind called positive stress or eustress.

This scale and its description were obtained, with permission to use, from Figley Institute's *Counterbalance the Intensity of Your Work: Compassion Stress Management Workbook*. Developer of the scale is in the footnotes.

Social Readjustment Rating Scale[20]

Instructions: Circle the number of any event which has occurred in your life over the past 12 months. Add up the numbers for your total score. When you are done, turn to the next page for score interpretation.

Event	Scale of Impact	Event	Scale of Impact
Death of spouse	100	Son or daughter leaving home	29
Divorce	73	Change in responsibility at work	29
Marital separation	65	Outstanding personal achievement	28
Jail term	63	Spouse begins/stops work	26
Death of close family member	63	Begin or end school	26
Personal injury or illness	53	Change in living conditions	25
Marriage	50	Revision of personal habits	24
Fired at work	47	Trouble with boss	23
Marital reconciliation	45	Change in work hours or conditions	20
Retirement	45	Change in residence	20

---

[20] T. H. Holmes and R. H. Rahe, "The Social Readjustment Rating Scale," *Journal of Psychosomatic Research*, 11(2), 213–221.

Change in health of family member	44	Change in schools	20
Pregnancy	39	Change in recreation	19
Sex difficulties	39	Change in church activity	19
Pain of new family member	39	Change in social activity	18
Business readjustment	39	Small mortgage or loan	17
Change in financial state	38	Change in sleep habits	16
Death of a close friend	37	Change in number of family get-togethers	15
Change to a different line of work	36	Change in eating habits	15
Change in number of arguments with spouse	35	Vacation	13
High mortgage	31	Christmas	12
Foreclosure of mortgage or loan	31	Minor violations of the law	11
Trouble with in-laws	29	**TOTAL SCORE**	

The Social Readjustment Rating Scale was designed to reflect the cumulative stress to which an individual has been exposed over a period of time (Holmes and Holmes, 1970; Holmes and Rahe, 1967; Rahe and Arthur, 1978). "Life change units" are used to measure life stress in the areas noted above.

Score Interpretation

Score	Interpretation
150–199	If your current level of stress continues and/or you do not adopt effective stress-management strategies, you have a **37% chance** of a **minor illness** in the next two years.
200–299	If your stress level continues and you do nothing to change your adaptive strategies, you have a **51% chance** of developing a **major illness** in the next two years.
>300	You have a **79% chance** of a **major health breakdown** in the next two years. It is recommended that you begin adding effective coping strategies to your lifestyle.

Mindful Living

> *The little things? The little moments? They aren't little.*
> —**Jon Kabat-Zinn,**
> American professor, writer,
> founder of Mindfulness-Based
> Stress Reduction Clinic
> (Goodreads.com)

This book is infused with suggestions on living mindfully, and this is especially important as we approach psychological self-care. *Mindfulness* is "the practice of experiencing reality in the present moment through awareness." According to Jon Kabat-Zinn, MD, some attitudinal factors that are important to experience mindfulness include slowing down, paying attention, and observing without judgment. It means, be here and in the now.[21]

---

[21] Jon Kabat-Zinn, *Full Catastrophe Living* (New York: Bantam Books, 2013), 66.

We often get caught in the stories cycling through our minds about past events or thinking about the future. We can learn from the past, but it is gone and does not serve us to dwell there. Thinking about the future can be helpful for the purpose of planning however can create fear and anxiety regarding the unknown. The future is not reality and has not yet happened. The present, the moment of here and now as it is experienced, is the only moment that is real.

Our minds wander and often can be found ruminating on anything but what is before us. Mindful living is about living in the moment with awareness and intention. It is about paying attention and walking through life with eyes wide open, rather than sleepwalking and missing what is actually happening. Easier said than done, but it can be accomplished with practice. We will talk more about this later in this chapter.

One can experience great peace and acceptance by living in the present moment. There are many gifts and much beauty missed in the present moment because we can find ourselves identifying with the stories played out in our minds regarding the past and/or future. This is part of the human condition, and there is no reason for self-judgment as the purpose of the mind is for thinking. Overidentification with our thoughts can be counterproductive as they are often driven by emotion and based upon opinions and judgments rather than on reality. Getting out of our minds and fully living in our bodies through experiencing is liberating.

Maintain Dual Focus

When we get too caught up in the busyness of the world, we lose connection with one another—and with ourselves.
—Jack Kornfield,
American author
(Goodreads.com)

Psychological self-care involves having a dual focus as you maneuver your life. This can be done by maintaining a connection and paying attention to what is going on within yourself while engaging with others and the world around you. As a Westerner, you have been socialized to put all your focus onto others and the external world. It is important not to lose sight of yourself while you are with others. Mindfulness practice helps one to remain connected to themselves, their bodily sensations, feelings, thoughts, and beliefs—being present with one's self while engaged with others and in activities. Maintaining a connection to your mind, body, and soul at all times will serve you well. It serves as your personal navigation system or inner compass, guiding you as you maneuver in the world. With this inner relationship, you will sense when something is wrong. When you need to change direction, it can guide you to safety. Having a mindful inner focus while engaging with others can foster self-awareness, and it can be a reminder not to take on the emotions of others.

Be Mindful of Your Feelings and Needs

As you cultivate a dual focus, pay attention to your feelings. Asking "How do I feel?" can help keep you in connection with yourself, until your relationship with your feelings becomes natural. Explore the feelings you get inside while associating with others or participating in activities. Notice if someone or something *triggers* an internal reaction or sensation within yourself. You will get a lot of information if you pay attention to what is happening around you and how it makes you feel inside. Doing so will give you feedback on areas to explore and heal. It is important not to judge the feelings you have, as they are natural and deserve to be sensed. Feeling it is the best way to heal or resolve it. More than the attention of anyone else, what we really crave is to be acknowledged and met by ourselves. It is in the acceptance of yourself and all your feelings that you heal and become whole. I will share more on this later in the chapter.

Another important question to ask yourself often is, "What do I need?" Many of us have been conditioned to push our needs down as if they are not important. Sometimes as children, when our needs did not get met, we stopped paying attention to them and giving them voice. If you notice that you feel off-center, ask yourself the question and see what answer you get. We often are disconnected from our needs or expect to have them fulfilled by someone or something outside ourselves. This powerful question will guide you to the self-care that you need. Some examples of needs not met that could make one feel off-center include need for nourishment, a break, time alone, to express one's self, movement, etc. If you get an answer that you cannot meet in that moment, be sure to have an inner dialogue stating that you will meet that need at a later time and then follow through.

While doing therapy at a women's shelter as a practicum student, the stories were unlike anything I had ever heard. It was unbelievable that anyone could withstand such abuse or that people on the planet were inflicting such pain on others. There was knowledge that this type of abuse existed, but it took things to a new level of awareness when victims were coming to me for help. It was shocking, and I felt so vulnerable as a new student witnessing such cruelty second-hand. Occasionally it felt like a lump in my throat would remain until the opportunity to cry came later that night. I acknowledged and held that part within myself that felt vulnerable near, almost imagining that I was carrying and nurturing the little girl inside.

Once the opportunity presented itself following work, I would fully experience that sadness and shed the tears that needed to be released. Sometimes this happened on the way from home or after the kids went to bed. At times, I felt like doing the happy dance because I finally had a moment to myself but was not willing to ignore or suppress the emotion from the day. On occasions like this, it helped to put in a sad movie like *Steel Magnolias* to get the tears flowing. The last thing I wanted was to end up with trapped emotional energy or depression because I did not deal with it.

If you are feeling off for no apparent reason, it is a good idea to ask yourself, "Is this mine or someone else's?" Sometimes people who are empathic sense the emotional energies of other people's as if they are their own. You may also figure it out by recalling how you felt prior to an interaction. For example, if you felt great before interacting with a coworker who was venting about how angry she is at her husband, and then you felt agitated following the interaction, chances are it is not yours. Once you recognize that the emotional energy is not yours, you simply set the intention to release it since it is not yours to deal with or send it back to its origin. This is an also an example about how awareness can help guide you. If your coworker carried on venting but you were not really paying attention to her or how you were feeling inside as she angrily vented, you might have missed the information you needed to figure out why you felt as you did and carried the energy all day. This is an example of how presence can serve well.

Relaxation Techniques

It is essential to incorporate relaxation techniques into your self-care practice. I recommend inserting these methods into your day-to-day living, wherever and whenever you can. Some tools only take a few minutes and can be squeezed in between clients, meetings, or activities at work. Others take more time and need to be done at home or in a more relaxing environment. This information is by no means all-inclusive but is shared to give you some ideas. You know better than anyone what relaxes you. It is helpful to have several options, as what is appropriate in one situation may not be appropriate in another. I encourage you to get creative with this and have fun.

Breath Work

Sometimes the most important thing we do in a whole day is the rest we take between two breaths.
—Etty Hillesum,
Dutch author *Wherever You are There You Are*
(Goodreads.com)

Intentional and focused breathing is the quickest way to induce the parasympathetic relaxation response. It is easy and can be done anywhere. You can even do it while you are at work listening to other people. Try these techniques for five minutes each:

1. Slowly inhale on a count of five, exhale on a count of five… repeat.
2. Slowly inhale on a count of five, hold for a count, slowly exhale on a count of five, hold for a count…repeat.
3. Slowly inhale on a count of five, slowly exhale on a count of ten…repeat.

The count can be adjusted to your comfort level, but for exercises 1 and 2, it should be even on the inhale/exhale, and for exercise 3, it should be twice as long as on the exhale. The abdomen should rise on the inhale (inflate) and fall (flatten) on the exhale. Your body will get more oxygen by breathing in this rhythm. Repeat the suggested patterns for as many minutes as you would like. These can be beneficial within just a few more minutes or be expanded out longer for a long meditation on the breath.

Meditation

Meditation can help us embrace our fear, our anger: and that is very healing. We let our natural capacity of healing do the work.
—Thich Nhat Hahn,
Zen master, spiritual teacher,
author (Brainyquote.com)

Meditation is recognized as a great stress-relief tool with vast and potentially life-altering benefits. Meditation can be done anywhere by anyone. It can be done while sitting, lying down, taking a shower, eating, cooking, walking, dancing, painting, writing, listening to music, praying, doing yoga, and the list goes on. Life can be a meditation if living is done mindfully by experiencing and being present moment by moment.

The benefits of meditation include, but are not limited to, reduced stress, elevation and maintenance of positive emotions, increased resilience, mind-body connection, greater awareness, self-reflection, clarity, acceptance of present moment reality, quiet mind, increased concentration, and greater creativity/imagination and connectedness to all that exists. Meditation has become the subject of study for neuroscientists, and there have been findings to support that meditation positively changes how the brain functions during stressful situations. Additionally, consistent meditation practice has been shown to restore health in people who experience pain and illness.

Compelling studies have been done to demonstrate the positive effects meditation has on the gray matter in the brain. One study used MRI brain scans to show how meditation for thirty minutes per day for eight weeks showed an increase in the gray matter in the brain, especially the hippocampus, the area responsible for memory and learning. The meditators had a decrease in the gray matter in the amygdala, the area of the brain associated with stress and anxiety. Additionally, those who meditated reported an increase in compassion. The control group showed no changes in their before and after MRI brain scan results.[22]

Tips for Beginning a Mindfulness Meditation Practice

Meditation may seem foreign or intimidating if you have never tried it. Learning to meditate is actually simple and can be as natural as breathing. For the sake of stress relief, the purpose is to calm the

---

[22] Brent Lambert, "Harvard Unveils MRI Study Proving Meditation Literally Rebuilds the Brain's Gray Matter in 8 Weeks," Feelguide, November 19, 2014, accessed August 1, 2020, https://www.feelguide.com/2014/11/19/harvard-unveils-mri-study-proving-meditation-literally-rebuilds-the-brains-gray-matter-in-8-weeks/.

mind and relax the body by inducing the parasympathetic relaxation response. The more often you do it, the better the results. Below are some tips to help you get started.

- Find some quiet time by yourself that will be uninterrupted. This could be in the morning before you get out of bed or in the evening before going to sleep.
- Get comfortable by sitting on a cushion, chair, or lying down on your back with your spine straight.
- Set the intention of *being* rather than *doing*. You can set other intentions such as letting go, giving your mind and body permission to relax, connecting with yourself, etc.
- Start by noticing your breath and how it feels in your chest, belly, nostrils, or wherever.
- Continue to focus on your breath, moment by moment and breath by breath.
- You may notice that your breath begins to change as you give it attention or that you begin to feel sensations in your body by giving it your awareness.
- You may notice your mind wandering, and if so, just notice without judgment as this is what minds do.
- This awareness and acceptance can assist with detaching from thoughts and prevent you from getting carried away by them.
- Observe what is going on and what you are experiencing, without judgment, for that is the moment of awareness.
- You can bring your awareness back to your breath over and over, as necessary.
- Initially, this practice can take time to get used to. It requires patience, self-compassion, and appreciation for attempting a new practice and taking the time to nurture yourself.
- When you are finished, ground yourself by bringing your awareness back to the room and into your body by noticing your feet on the ground and how your body feels as you move.

- Following guided meditations can be helpful and relaxing as you begin a practice. For your convenience, complimentary guided meditation downloads can be found at www.selfcarespecialists.com or www.blossomingheartcenter.com.

	Strategies for Inducing Relaxation Response[23]			
	Breath Work	Meditation	Progressive Relaxation	Visualization/ Guided Imagery
Anxiety	X	X	X	X
Chronic pain	X	X	X	X
Depression	X	X	X	
Fatigue	X		X	
Headaches/ Migraine headaches	X	X	X	X
High blood pressure	X	X	X	
Insomnia	X		X	
Irritability	X	X	X	X
Muscle tension	X		X	X

---

[23] Charles R. Figley, "*Counterbalance the Intensity of Your Work: Compassion Stress Management Participant Workbook*". (Tallahassee: Figley Institute), 40.

Meditation purifies and strengthens your heart. It steadies your nerves. It augments the brain power.
—**Sri Swami Sivananda,**
spiritual teacher,
(Azquotes.com)

Forms of Creative Expression

Forms of creative expression can be like moving meditations, as they engage us in the presence of enjoying artistic expression. There are countless forms of creative expression, including imaginative writing, reading, writing poetry, dancing, drawing, painting, sculpting, playing music, singing, humming, gardening, decorating, designing, taking photographs, and beyond. If you are not sure where to start, think about what you enjoyed doing as a child. It might be fun to bring that talent back into your life. Another option is to take a class in something you always wanted to do but did not. It is never too late to learn, and sometimes we can really appreciate engaging in inspired expression even more as an adult. A few years ago, I enrolled in a salsa dance class. I was terrible, but it sure was fun to try and served as good excuse for socializing.

Journaling / Mind Mapping / Letter Writing

It can be very therapeutic to write down our thoughts in a journal. Sometimes we just need to get them out of our heads and onto paper. In the process of doing so, it is also possible to have emotional releases. It can also be insightful to read past journal entries to see how progress was made. This can help us realize that the problems of today are just a moment in time. It is a great foundation for personal growth. It serves as a wonderful mirror to witness your life as you write. All you need is some quiet time and a book or something to type on. It is an excellent medium to express your thoughts, feelings, questions, beliefs, dreams, and beyond.

You may also benefit from mind mapping. A mind map is a way to get information out of your head and onto paper. You can use words, symbols, lines, colors, and pictures. It can be used to write down ideas, feelings, pictures, and words that help you express yourself. It can be valuable in making connections between events, circumstances, and people. I have found mind mapping to be effective to express difficult emotions like anger. When everything is expressed by writing on paper, it is therapeutic and freeing to tear it to shreds or burn it.

Writing a letter to someone you are frustrated with and then not sending it can also be great stress relief. Perhaps there are some things you would like to say, but it would jeopardize the relationship. The ability to honestly express yourself and everything you are feeling can help get things off your chest. I do recommend destroying the letter once you are finished. After you simmer down, you may get clarity regarding whether or not you need to speak your truth about the situation and how to do so in a way that honors both yourself and the other person.

Spend Time in Nature / Outdoor Activities

We can become so busy with our indoor work and responsibilities that we forget that the outdoors exists. This is unfortunate because spending time in nature can be very grounding, relaxing, and rejuvenating. Nurturing nature time can assist us to gain positive perspective and feel like a true reprieve from the demands of life. Outdoor activities are limitless and can include walking in nature, running outdoors, sitting by a fire, soaking up the sun, swimming, walking on the beach, hiking, boating, biking, camping, playing outdoor games, having fun at the park, bird-watching, dog-walking, gardening, etc. I have even found myself enjoying yard work like raking leaves because being outdoors is a refreshing change with the sunshine, fresh air, clear energy, fragrant scents, and spaciousness.

Listen to Tranquil Sounds and Music

This can be accomplished by spending time outside and being mindful of the sounds around you such as birds chirping, wind chimes, the waves of the ocean, leaves blowing in the wind, children playing, and more. You can also listen to soothing vibrations through music. It is relaxing and peaceful listening to music that incorporates sounds such as ocean waves, rain, birds chirping, and others. You can unwind after work by playing this in your car on the way home, hearing the music softly playing while taking a bath, upon waking (much kinder than the alarm clock), during meditation, and while doing other relaxing activities.

Everything has vibration, including music and sounds. Music has been shown to affect various centers in the brain. So choose wisely and with intention. The peaceful tones and sounds cultivate peace and calm. Classical music can boost creativity and thinking. In contrast, hyper songs can rev you up. Heavy metal has been demonstrated to have negative effects on the frontal lobe of the brain. Music can resonate with us deeply and can be very healing if chosen well. Music with binaural beats is often used in conjunction with therapy sessions, massage, yoga, and other healing modalities.

Positive Thinking and Attitude of Gratitude

The greatest weapon against stress is our ability to choose one thought over another.
—William James,
American philosopher
and psychologist,
(Brainyquote.com)

Positive thinking not only helps us to feel optimistic but has a beneficial effect on the world around us. We can choose to look at the bright side of things and the growth that each situation brings or focus on the negative aspects of life. Where your attention goes, the energy flows. With this in mind, it is advisable to keep your perspective positive and light. It does not mean ignoring how you feel, as suppressing feelings can have long-term, deleterious effects. It requires being aware of your thoughts and noticing how they can cultivate negative feelings within. Yes, your thoughts can make you feel bad. When negative feelings are triggered within, it is important to acknowledge these and work through them. You just do not want to remain stuck in them.

Have you ever noticed that when you wake up thinking it's going to be a great day, with a skip in your step, that things seem to go better and people around you respond with more kindness. Or that when you dwell on something that goes wrong, more negative occurrences appear? Imagine that your thoughts are a magnet and attract the reality to you that you have projected out into the world. Yes, you are that powerful! It is a good reason to have awareness regarding your thoughts, keeping them kind and positive as much as possible. If your thinking is negative and you are unable to maintain an optimistic perspective, this is a strong indication that you may benefit from the assistance of a trained professional.

It has been said that "what we resist persists." If you are avoiding looking within yourself for the root of the problem, it will persist. In fact, sometimes it gets bigger and bigger until there is no choice to look at it. It may seem easier to avoid it, but this is actually the hard way.

I highly encourage having an attitude of gratitude. While there are negative aspects of life that we must deal with, there are always things that we can appreciate about our lives. Focusing on that which is going well tends to usher in more positive energy. I have literally felt how my energetic vibration raises by feeling gratitude in my heart for the blessings in my life. Sometimes these are simple, like gratitude for the food I eat, for hot water (especially after the hot water heater broke), for a safe home, a comfortable bed to sleep in, etc. During times of financial stress, I have found it especially important to be grateful for the abundance in my life. During tough times, gratitude is essential to keeping a positive attitude. Having a gratitude journal is a great way to ponder and express gratitude for the positive aspects of life.

An ongoing attitude of gratitude is most ideal as you will attract more abundance from a place of appreciating what you have rather than focusing on what you lack. If you want to be more abundant, acknowledge what you have and sense the feeling of abundance within. Feel the sensations in your body of what it would feel like if you already have that which you are desiring. This is a powerful way to draw it into your reality. You can add visualization and gratitude for it as if it is already here. It is great way to place your order to the Universe and then trust that it is on the way! This is based on the universal principle of the law of attraction. Additionally, it is important to take action steps toward your chosen destination, even if they are baby steps.

Use Your Sense of Humor and Laugh Often

Sometimes we take life way too seriously. Having a sense of humor as you go through life can be most advantageous. There is often something humorous even in the most difficult situations. Shifting your perspective to incorporate lightness and humor can help soften challenging conditions and ease stress. It is a form of letting go. You have a choice to let things weigh you down or keep them light. Even the most serious circumstances are a moment in time that too shall pass, so wherever you can find humor, I recommend finding it.

One of the signs of burnout is when someone has lost his or her sense of humor. When someone reaches a point of burnout, it is often time to make a change such as working less hours, shifting responsibilities, taking a leave, or changing jobs. Additionally, doing some inner work would be beneficial.

I encourage spending time with people who you enjoy and laugh with. Try putting light and fun activities into your life like hilarious movies, karaoke, a special trip to a comedy club, humorous YouTube videos, game night, and the like. Laughing is very therapeutic and can release stress in amazing ways. There are even therapists who facilitate laugh therapy, clown therapy, and happiness coaching. None of which I have researched or experienced, but I have met a few who say that it really helps their clients. We all deserve to be happy and joyful, which can be cultivated through laughter. Let your inner child out to play and get silly!

Vacation, Staycation, and Weekend Getaway

Scheduling time off for vacation, staycation, or weekend getaways can be essential in preventing burnout. Charles Figley stated, "Burnout is a progressive loss of idealism, energy, and goals as the result of personal or occupational stress. Burnout results from high levels of stress over time. Continuing personal or work stress, without rest, will eventually lead to burnout."[24]

Getting a break from the demands of life, both professional and personal, can be necessary. Sometimes we need a change of scenery to let go, rejuvenate, and gain fresh perspective. This can often be accomplished by scheduling time off from work and away from home. It is best to plan respite before reaching the point of frustration and exhaustion. Vacation to a new destination, a favorite place previously visited, a workshop or retreat, visiting out-of-town family and/or friends could be exactly the break you are needing.

If you have some paid time off but cannot financially afford a vacation away from home, I recommend the *staycation*. Spending vacation time at home can also be a refreshing break. Time off may seem extended by *unplugging* for a while by taking a break from email and silencing the cell phone. Letting people know in advance that you will be doing so is a good idea. Setting boundaries around your time can give a sense of freedom and relaxation. Giving yourself permission to do what you want to do, moment by moment, and without an agenda during your leave is a wonderful gift to yourself.

---

[24] Charles R. Figley, *Counterbalance the Intensity of Your Work: Compassion Stress Management Participant Workbook* (Tallahassee: Figley Institute, 2013), 5.

If time off from work is not an option, you may also get a nice break by scheduling a weekend getaway trip. A quick change of environment can have similar relaxing and refreshing effects as a vacation. The same intentions as the staycation mentioned above could be done during a weekend at home. Sometimes saying "not now" or "no" to others and "yes" to yourself is necessary self-care. You will have more to give others when you tend to your needs and rejuvenate yourself. By giving from this place, everyone benefits.

Avoid the Use of Alcohol to Manage Stress

Under stressful circumstances, many people turn to alcohol to cope. Alcoholic drinks are often consumed to "take off the edge" or "relax" after a long, hard day of work. While this may seem to help in the moment, it pushes the emotions one is experiencing below consciousness or awareness. It is difficult to resolve feelings that have been repressed, and these can build up if the pattern of repression is habitual. Repeated alcohol consumption to manage stress can lead to addiction, which can have severe consequences affecting every area of one's life.

Those who are experiencing personal trauma and/or secondary trauma through their work, family relationships, or socially may be especially vulnerable to misuse of alcohol to mask painful emotions. The moments when an individual most feels like they need a drink are often the worst time for a drink.

It is a good practice to be mindful when you feel the urge to consume alcohol. Good questions to ask yourself are "Why do I feel the need to drink right now?" and "What activity could I engage in that would be better for my health?" Examples of healthy alternatives can include exercise, mindfulness meditation, breath work, taking a relaxing bath, journaling, or seeking social support.

The ability to meet yourself where you are, regardless of how difficult it may seem in the moment, is a skill worth mastering. If you do not like where you are, it is a good indication that you need to do something different, nurture yourself and/or perhaps seek some support or assistance to work through the stress. This can be done by talking with a trusted friend, coworker, life coach, support group, or therapist. More involved help may be necessary if you suspect an alcohol addiction.

I was facilitating a Compassion Stress Management course for professional caregivers a few years ago and had a participant walk out in the middle of the class. A few days later, I received an email from this individual that something I said had inspired her to leave and find an Alcoholics Anonymous group that was meeting in that city (she was from out of town) immediately. This was an excellent example of self-awareness, courage, and doing what she found necessary to cultivate a healthier, addiction-free lifestyle.

Find Outlets for Anger and Other Difficult Emotions

We plant the seeds that will flower as results in our lives, so best to remove the weeds of anger, avarice, envy, and doubt that peace and abundance may manifest for all.
—**Dorothy Day,** American journalist and social activist
(Inspiringquotes.us)

Some emotions are more difficult to express than others. Anger, in particular, can be very damaging to one's self if it is held within. It is especially important to have outlets that help you release this sometimes-explosive energy. It is imperative that you do not harm yourself, other humans, animals, properties, or valuable objects as you purge heavy emotions. I recommend that you use your intention to connect with and feel the emotion as you engage in the outlet. By doing this, you are more likely to release it in the process. There is a holistic health center in my city that has a wall in which clients can throw skeet to encourage the release of emotions. Here are a few examples of outlets for releasing anger and difficult emotions.

- Shoot a toy or real bow and arrow (with the target being the emotion you desire to feel and release, *not* a picture of the person you are angry with)
- Throw damp tissues at the garage wall or ceiling
- Throw tennis balls at the outside of your garage door
- Play tennis or racquetball
- Hit a cardboard box with a soft whiffle ball bat
- Throw stones into a field or body of water

Sometimes we just need a few minutes to vent with a trusted friend or confidant. It is helpful to have people in your life who support and love you unconditionally. I recommend trying to process difficult feelings with your personal tools first if possible, as you do not want to release negative energy all over the people you care about (or anyone for that matter). Trained professionals understand how to work with challenging emotions and objectively help without taking them on. Keep in mind that your family and loved ones really care about you and are more likely to be disturbed and personally engaged as you share. If your relationship with someone becomes a continual dumping ground for your issues, it is likely to strain the relationship and become toxic for the other.

Utilize Counseling and Therapy Services

It takes courage to grow up and become who you really are.
—EE Cummings
(Brainyquote.com)

I will never forget the day I gave one of my first continuing-education seminars for a large group of mental health professionals and one of the most experienced therapists said, "Every good therapist has a therapist." There was so much truth in that statement. It would be beneficial for anyone and everyone to have a good therapist. We all have times in our lives that are challenging, overwhelming, and exhausting. Sometimes we just need a little extra help getting through a situation or difficult time period. People often avoid seeing a therapist because they perceive needing help as a sign of weakness. It actually takes a lot of courage to face our inner pain, deepest fears, insecurities, regrets, and so on. Trained professionals can help us navigate these feelings and scenarios quickly and gracefully.

I highly recommend finding a therapist who utilizes deeper methods to aid in self-discovery and healing rather than "talk therapy." While there is some therapeutic benefit to talking and thinking about an issue, deep healing usually occurs when we access the root of the problem. Our current life situations and stressors often trigger held emotions and beliefs formed during earlier times in our lives. Quite often, but not always, the trigger goes back to the formative years, between ages birth to seven. During our younger years, we were not equipped mentally or emotionally to process our experiences, particularly traumatic or abusive encounters. Many well-intentioned people in our lives and, some without good intentions, caused harm due to their lack of awareness.

Some therapy modalities I have found to be the most effective include body-centered therapies, mind-body therapies, and subconscious-belief repatterning methods. They often get to the root of the problem, helping the client to release the emotional energy and belief embedded at the time of initial upset or trauma. The body-centered approaches I recommend include Hakomi body-centered psychotherapy, Sensory Motor Psychotherapy, and Somatic Experiencing. EMDR (Eye Movement Desensitization Reprocessing) is a mind-body therapy that has been well-researched related to healing trauma. My two favorite subconscious-belief repatterning therapies include Psych-K and Emotional Freedom Technique. Additionally, the Neuro-Emotional Technique is a helpful healing tool used to find and remove neurological imbalances caused by unresolved emotions. Hypnosis can be helpful in accessing information from the subconscious to be transformed. I suggest finding a practitioner that uses one or a combination of these methods.

By doing deep work, we uncover and transform held emotions, beliefs, sabotaging patterns, and unhealthy coping mechanisms. These methods help us access the information and transform it through understanding, acceptance, and self-compassion. Some people do this work because they need to heal anxiety, depression, trauma, and other emotional issues. Others are led to do this work because they desire assistance with personal discovery, growth, and self-actualization. Doing the work is very freeing and allows us to live fuller, richer lives.

I have found that doing deeper emotional work with the modalities previously mentioned resolves issues more quickly and deeply than talk therapy or cognitive behavior therapy. My clients often report that they got more healing from one to two sessions with me compared to what they achieved through years of talk therapy. When working with clients, my goal is not to keep them coming for long periods of time, but to guide them toward deep healing so they are empowered to navigate life successfully and have the skills to resolve difficult emotions as they are experienced. Depending on the severity of the issue/s experienced, clients usually come up to once a week for a month and then less often (once or twice a month) until they get to the as-needed basis. Most of my clients come once a month for maintenance or as needed during times of an occasional crisis. Some clients remove their emotional/mental blockages and achieve their goals within just a few sessions.

It has been amazing to witness how the physical ailments of my clients often resolve when they do body-centered psychotherapy. It makes sense, as the emotional energy is stored in the physical body, which can cause disturbances that cause pain and illness. Through school and a variety of workshops, I have heard that anywhere from 85–100 percent of physical issues are caused by unresolved emotions. It is my belief, from the experiences in my practice, that there is an emotional element in most illnesses. The word *disease* breaks down into "dis" "ease" and means lack of ease. Illness is a disorder of structure or function within a human, especially, illnesses that produce specific signs or symptoms that affect a specific location and is not simply a direct result of physical injury.

Some of the physical issues that have been resolved within my therapy and/or emotional energy-healing practices include chronic acid reflux, irritable bowel syndrome, digestive issues, fibromyalgia, migraines, chronic pain from previous accidents, and vertigo to name a few. The clients with these issues had addressed them with traditional Western medical doctors without the relief they were seeking. Many of my clients come off medications prescribed for depression, anxiety, high blood pressure, sleep disorders, pain, and beyond when they do their deep emotional work. The need for these disappears when the root of the problem is addressed.

I usually do subconscious belief work with clients who have emotional and physical ailments. An important aspect of healing is the belief that our minds and bodies are capable of healing and that we are worthy of being healthy. Our beliefs often dictate our reality, so it is important that they are life-affirming. We are only aware of a small percentage of these. A large percentage of our beliefs are subconscious or beneath our awareness. The percentage depends on how aware the individual is, but even a highly aware individual may only be conscious of 20 percent of his/her beliefs. This figure goes down with less mindful individuals. Muscle testing can be used to test for subconscious beliefs and then corrected with subconscious-belief repatterning modalities, such as Psych-K (psychology plus kinesiology).

When seeking help with your inner journey, it is important to find a professional who has a commitment to both his/her inner work and the healing of others. One can guide others better from a place of personal experience and proficiency. It's been said that a practitioner can take clients only as deep as he/she is willing to go within himself/herself. If the clinician has done deep inner work, he or she will have the ability to be very present with you during the session and likely embody the healing qualities of understanding, nonjudgment, and compassion. As a result of this embodiment, the practitioner should be able to guide you toward presence, understanding, compassion, and love toward yourself.

Energy Healing

If therapy or counseling is not your style, there are other healing professionals who may resonate with you. Possibilities include a life coach, shaman, energy healer, ordained minister, etc. I have found inner-child healing, soul retrieval, and past-life regression to be valuable in accessing information and deep healing as well. Energy medicine is up and coming, healing psychological and physical issues with specific energy frequencies, through frequency technology or hands-on healing.

I offer hands-on healing through Blossoming Heart Center as an ordained minister of healing, and my clients have experienced profound results. Examples of the results include disappearance of chronic pain, return of sensation in areas where it had disappeared, and resolution of acute and chronic health problems of varying degrees. This work was done both in person and remotely from a distance. The results are not something that I can guarantee because I channel the energy of source, higher vibrational archangels, ascended masters, spirit guides, and healers. I attribute the healing to these high vibrational beings, the energy they channel, and the innate capability the individual has to heal. I simply serve as a clear channel for which they work through. God and Divine Spirit can heal things that sometimes cannot be explained by Western medicine and are simply miraculous. The work is multidimensional and can positively influence individuals on the physical, mental, emotional, and spiritual levels.

Personal growth and flourishing can occur following the experiencing of an event/s that could be considered traumatic. This scale was obtained, with permission to use, by Figley Institute in *Counterbalance the Intensity of Your Work: Compassion Stress Management Workbook*.

Posttraumatic Growth Inventory—Short Form[25]

Before answering the following questions, focus on one traumatic or life-altering event that has occurred in your life. Please circle the general experience you are thinking of:

Loss of a loved one	Disaster	Accident or injury
Chronic or acute illness	Job loss	Divorce
Violent or abusive crime	Financial hardship	Retirement
Change in family responsibility	Career or location change/move	Combat Other

Circle time elapsed since event occurred.

6 months–1 year   1–2 years   2–5 years   More than 5 years

Indicate for the statement below the degree to which the change reflected in the question is true in your life as a result of your crisis, using the following scale. Responses are made on the following six-point scale:

0 = I did not experience this change as a result of my crisis.

1 = I experienced this change to a very small degree as a result of my crisis.

2 = I experienced this change to a small degree as a result of my crisis.

3 = I experienced this change to a moderate degree as a result of my crisis.

4 = I experienced this change to a great degree as a result of my crisis.

5 = I experienced this change to a very great degree as a result of my crisis.

---

[25] Arnie Cann, Lawrence G. Calhoun, Richard G. Tedeschi, Kanako Taku, Tanya Vishnevsky, Kelli N. Triplett, and Suzanne C. Danhauer, "A Short Form of the Posttraumatic Growth Inventory," *Anxiety, Stress & Coping*, 23: 2, 127–137.

1. I changed my priorities about what is important in life.	0	1	2	3	4	5
2. I have a greater appreciation for the value of my own life.	0	1	2	3	4	5
3. I am able to do better things with my life.	0	1	2	3	4	5
4. I have a better understanding of spiritual matters.	0	1	2	3	4	5
5. I have a greater sense of closeness with others.	0	1	2	3	4	5
6. I established a new path for my life.	0	1	2	3	4	5
7. I know better that I can handle difficulties.	0	1	2	3	4	5
8. I have a stronger religious faith.	0	1	2	3	4	5
9. I discovered that I'm stronger than I thought I was.	0	1	2	3	4	5
10. I learned a great deal about how wonderful people are.	0	1	2	3	4	5

Scoring Instructions

	Area of Growth	Items	Score
I.	Relating to others	5 10	
II.	New possibilities	3 6	
III.	Personal strength	7 9	
IV.	Spiritual change	4 8	
V.	Appreciation of life	1 2	
		Total	

Practice Self-Compassion

*Our sorrows and wounds
are only healed when we touch
them with compassion.*
—Buddha
(Goodreads.com)

One of the most essential things you can do for your personal well-being and healing is to be compassionate with yourself. We are all humans who experience challenges in varying degrees. We can be our own worst critics when what we really need is to befriend ourselves with understanding, acceptance, compassion, and love. This can be challenging to do if you have conscious or subconscious beliefs regarding not being good enough, low self-worth, low self-esteem, or are self-critical and have perfectionistic tendencies.

According to self-compassion expert Dr. Kristin Neff, "Having compassion for yourself means that you honor and accept your humanness. Things will not always go the way you want them to. You will encounter frustrations, losses will occur, you will make mistakes, bump up against your limitations, or fall short of your ideas. This is the human condition, a reality shared by all of us. The more you open your heart to this reality instead of constantly fighting against it, the more you will be able to feel compassion for yourself and all your fellow humans in the experience of life."[26]

The most powerful healer you will ever find is the healer within yourself. The power of compassion and love cannot be underestimated. Healing occurs when we consistently treat ourselves with gentleness, love, and compassion. That is what I love about the work I do! I do not do the healing work for my clients but guide them

---

[26] Kristin Neff, "The Three Elements of Self-Compassion," Self-Compassion.org, accessed August 15, 2020, https://self-compassion.org/the-three-elements-of-self-compassion-2/. Permission to use granted.

toward the healing resources within themselves. Many need help accessing these resources for themselves, which is understandable given that self-care and self-love are new paradigms in the Western world.

Included on the next few pages is a self-assessment regarding self-compassion, which can be insightful. If your self-compassion is not where you prefer it to be, take note that this is an area to work toward improving within yourself. Kristin Neff, PhD, the developer of the Self-Compassion Scale, is considered the leading expert on self-compassion. She has written several books and offers training workshops regarding self-compassion. You will find titles of the books in appendix/recommended reading at the end of the book. She does offer several free resources including complimentary meditations and exercises on her website www.self-compassion.org.

This scale was obtained with permission to use from Figley Institute's *Counterbalance the Intensity of Your Work: Compassion Stress Management Workbook and developer Kristin Neff, PhD.*

Self-Compassion Scale[27]

Instructions: Please read each statement carefully before answering. To the right of each item, indicate how often you behave in the stated manner, using the following scale:

Almost Never	Occasionally	About Half the Time	Fairly Often	Almost Always
1	2	3	4	5

		1	2	3	4	5
1.	I'm disapproving and judgmental about my own flaws and inadequacies.					

---

[27] *Counterbalance the Intensity of Your Work: Compassion Stress Management Participant Workbook.* (Tallahassee: Figley Institute, 2013), 18.

		1	2	3	4	5
2.	When I'm feeling down, I tend to obsess and fixate on everything that's wrong.					
3.	When things are going badly for me, I see the difficulties as part of life that everyone goes through.					
4.	When I think about my inadequacies, it tends to make me feel more separate and cut off from the rest of the world.					
5.	I try to be loving toward myself when I'm feeling emotional pain.					
6.	When I fail at something important to me I become consumed by feelings of inadequacy.					
7.	When I'm down and out, I remind myself that there are lots of other people in the world feeling like I am.					
8.	When times are really difficult, I tend to be tough on myself.					
9.	When something upsets me, I try to keep my emotions in balance.					
10.	When I feel inadequate in some way, I try to remind myself that feelings of inadequacy are shared by most people.					
11.	I'm intolerant and impatient toward those aspects of my personality I don't like.					
12.	When I'm going through a very hard time, I give myself the caring and tenderness I need.					
13.	When I'm feeling down, I tend to feel like most other people are probably happier than I am.					

		1	2	3	4	5
14.	When something painful happens, I try to take a balanced view of the situation.					
15.	I try to see my failings as part of the human condition.					
16.	When I see aspects of myself that I don't like, I get down on myself.					
17.	When I fail at something important to me, I try to keep things in perspective.					
18.	When I'm really struggling, I tend to feel like other people must be having an easier time of it.					
19.	I'm kind to myself when I'm experiencing suffering.					
20.	When something upsets me, I get carried away with my feelings.					
21.	I can be a bit cold-hearted toward myself when I'm experiencing suffering.					
22.	When I'm feeling down, I try to approach my feelings with curiosity and openness.					
23.	I'm tolerant of my own flaws and inadequacies.					
24.	When something painful happens, I tend to blow the incident out of proportion.					
25.	When I fail at something that is important to me, I tend to feel alone in my failure.					
26.	I try to be understanding and patient toward those aspects of my personality I do not like.					

To Whom It May Concern:

Please feel free to use the Self-Compassion Scale in your research. You can email me with any questions you may have. I would also ask that you please email me about any results you obtain with the scale and would appreciate it if you send me a copy of any article published using the scale. The appropriate reference is listed below.

Best,
Kristin Neff, PhD, Associate Professor
Educational Psychology Department
University of Texas at Austin
1 University Station, D5800
Austin, Texas, 78712
email: kristin.neff@mail.utexas.edu
Ph: (512) 471-0382   Fax: (512) 471-1288
Reference: Neff, K. D. (2003). Development and validation of a scale to measure self-compassion. *Self and Identity*, 2, 223–250.

Score Interpretation

Total Mean Score	1–2.5	2.5–3.5	3.5–5.0
Level of Self-Compassion	Low Self-Compassion	Moderate Self-Compassion	High Self-Compassion

Coding Key

Subscales[28]	Items	Mean Score
Self-Kindness	5	
"Being warm and	12	
understanding	19	
toward ourselves	23	
when we suffer,	26	
fail, or feel inade-		
quate, rather		
than ignoring		
our pain or		
flagellating		
ourselves with		
self-criticism."		
Self-Judgment	1	
(reverse score)	8	
	11	
	16	
	21	

Subscale scores are computed by calculating the mean of subscale item responses.

To compute a total self-compassion score, **reverse score** the negative subscale items—self-judgment, isolation, and over-identification (i.e., 1 = 5, 2 = 4, 3 = 3. 4 = 2, 5 = 1) - then compute a total mean.

(This method of calculating the total score is slightly different from what was used in the article referenced above, in which each subscale was added together. However, I find it is easier to interpret the scores if the total mean is used (K. Neff).

---

[28] Expanded subscale definitions can be found at http://www.self-compassion.org/what-is-self-compassion/the-three-elements-of-self-compassion.html.

Common   3
Humanity   7
"Recognizing   10
that suffering 15
and personal
inadequacy
is part of the
shared human
experience—
something that
we all go through
rather than
being something
that happens
to *me* alone."

Isolation   4
(reverse score) 13
                18
                25

Mindfulness   9
"A nonjudg-   14
mental, recep- 17
tive mind   22
state in which
one observes
thoughts and
feelings as they
are, without try-
ing to suppress
or deny them."

Over-identified	2
(reverse score)	6
	20
	24

Total Mean Score

Summary

Psychological self-care is an essential dimension of wellness and is deeply impactful in our moment-to-moment experience. It is important to be mindful and maintain a connection with yourself as you maneuver in a world that seems to be very other focused. We must acknowledge and satisfy our needs to maintain resiliency during day-to-day living and stressful times. Incorporating relaxation techniques such as breath work, meditation, forms of creative expression, journaling, spending time in nature, enjoying outdoor activities, and listening to tranquil sounds and peaceful music can be helpful to ease stress. Positive thinking and maintaining an attitude of gratitude can assist us in maintaining healthy perspective and creating a desirable reality. It is helpful to have a sense of humor and laugh often rather than taking life too seriously. Scheduled time off can give us the respite and rejuvenation necessary to keep going and aids in burnout prevention. When life gets to be too much or you desire personal growth, it is advantageous to engage in therapy or counseling resources. Approaching yourself with gentleness, understanding and compassion eases the human journey. Psychological self-care is the key to well-being and experiencing life to its fullest.

CHAPTER 5

Social/Interpersonal Self-Care

Thousands of candles can be lit from a single candle, and the light of the candle will not be shortened. Happiness never decreases by being shared.
—**Buddha** (Goodreads.com)

As human beings, we are wired to connect with others. Having healthy social and interpersonal relationships is an integral dimension of self-care. Some people tend toward introversion and others are more extroverted. Regardless of your social disposition, it is healthy to have people to connect with whether you have a small circle of trusted friends and family or a large social circle. Associations with others through healthy relationships can help us maintain balance. Some of the worst sensations we can experience as human beings are feelings of loneliness, separation, and isolation. Feeling as if no one understands us, cares about us, or loves us is a dark and sad place. This can lead to depression, anxiety, and even suicidal thoughts. Social and interpersonal self-care is an area to explore as it can help prevent the mentioned problems. I encourage you to take an honest inventory regarding where you are at within your relationships and social encounters.

A survey done by the AARP recently found that one in three adults aged forty-five and older report suffering from loneliness. According to research done by psychologist and neuroscientist Julianne Holt-Lunstad of Brigham Young University, adults who feel socially isolated have a 50 percent greater likelihood of dying from any cause within a given time frame than those who feel connected socially. She says, "Social connections have long been linked to indicators of health. We're simply social creatures."[29]

If you have difficulty relating with others and developing relationships, I recommend doing some inner work to connect more deeply with yourself. By developing a positive and healthy relationship with yourself, you are more likely to connect well with other people. According to Louise Hay, author and pioneer of "mirror work," the quality of your relationship with yourself influences the quality of your relationship with everyone and everything else. Additionally, she wrote that we date on our own level of self-esteem. Your capacity to love yourself helps you to recognize when others love you and makes it easier for others to love you. Your capacity to love yourself enables you to love others unconditionally.[30] Surely this applies to relationships with friends, families, colleagues, and others.

Develop Supportive Relationships

It is healthy to have relationships with people we trust and enjoy. These connections can be with intimate partners, friends, parents, siblings, your children, extended family, neighbors, colleagues, and within social circles. Taking the time to seek and cultivate meaningful relationships is highly recommended. If you reflect on your life and realize that you do not have enough people you can talk to, enjoy spending time with or that you can relate to, it may be time to find opportunities for socializing. People are everywhere. Sometimes we have got to get out of our comfort zone and make ourselves available

[29] Kluger, Jeffrey. "How Well Are You Really?" *New York Times* Special Edition on Wellness, February 15, 2019, p. 7.

[30] Louise Hay, "What Is Mirror Work?" LouiseHay.com, accessed July 8, 2019, https://www.louisehay.com/what-is-mirror-work/.

to new people and opportunities for interaction. In the following sections, I will give you some ideas of how to enhance your social and interpersonal self-care.

Know How and When to Get Help

It requires self-awareness to know how and when to get help. When our problems seem overwhelming, are on-going, and our capacity to cope diminishes, it is time to reach out for some assistance. Some see this as a sign of weakness, but it takes courage to get honest about feelings of helplessness, overwhelm and despair, among others. As humans, we have a broad range of emotions. Sometimes we feel as if we are the only ones having these experiences, as if we are different or somehow defective. The truth is, we all experience these sensations at some point in our lives, and we are more similar than different.

There are times when we need to ask for support or advice from people in our social circle whom we trust, and sometimes it is necessary to seek professional assistance. Help from others can be as simple as a friend or loved one serving as a sounding board who can offer suggestions or seeking out therapy to help get you out of a rut. Resources can vary depending on your needs. Get in touch with your personal requirements by asking yourself questions like the following:

- What do I need?
- Who would have knowledge or experience regarding my situation?
- Who can I trust to listen or give advice?

Participate in Social Groups

Spending time with people who share similar interests can be very meaningful. Participating in social groups with people who are like-minded and like-hearted can be a great opportunity to meet others who share in your values, beliefs, and activities. Often social groups have a purpose or a cause that brings people together, uniting and working toward a common goal. There are tribes, groups, associations, organizations, and societies dedicated to particular interests or activities everywhere. Whatever your pursuits are would be an area to research social groups available. These may be found within your area, or it might be possible to connect with people from abroad through travel or technology (social media, webinars, etc.).

Girls' or Guys' Night Out

There are times when we just need to get out and have fun. Scheduling outings with your friends, family, and coworkers is a great opportunity for connection, fun, and entertainment. Time out with the girls or guys can be uplifting whether it is with your closest friend/s or a larger group. There are so many options of things to do, including eating at restaurants; going to movies; watching sports events and televised games; attending book clubs, dinner clubs; watching concerts, plays, theater; going to comedy clubs; dancing; shopping, etc. These fun nights out can be spontaneous or scheduled.

Spend Time with Pets

Beloved pets can be an important aspect of social self-care as the relationships with them can be as nourishing as those with friends and family. They are amazing companions who love us unconditionally, and no matter how we show up, they greet us with love, affection, and attention. Our furry friends help keep us active as we walk and play with them. Pets remind us to be playful because they can be so silly, engaging, and adorable. They help us gain perspective when we are down. Animals help us be more present in the moment as their presence is obvious and contagious. They give us purpose and keep us caring about another or others during tough times.

An article was written by Dr. David Sack in *Psychology Today* regarding how dogs can serve as *nature's antidepressant* because they help us release the love hormone oxytocin, which plays a critical role in the formation of emotional bonds. In studies, it was shown to increase in both dogs and humans when they gazed into one another's eyes. Below are some findings that were discovered in the analysis of nearly seventy dog studies.

- Nursing homes with a live-in or visiting dog reported a decrease in depression among elderly residents.
- Children with psychiatric disorders showed improved mood regulation within just one therapy session with a dog.
- Pets were found to be a stabilizing factor for empty-nest couples.
- Long-term care patients who had interactions with dogs experienced less loneliness, and the effect was increased as they had more one-on-one time with the dog.
- Dogs act as a *social catalyst* while in a group by increasing smiles, conversation, and elevating moods during interaction.[31]

Summary

Because human beings are wired to connect, it is essential to have meaningful relationships to meet our basic needs. If you find communicating and relating well with others to be an issue, it is advisable to do some inner work to strengthen the relationship with yourself. Social and interpersonal self-care is key as it can help prevent loneliness, depression, isolation, and feelings of separation. Cultivating trusted partnerships does take some time and effort; however, it is so worth it because you will enjoy an increase in overall well-being and quality of life.

---

[31] David Sack, "Nature's Antidepressant: The Dog," *Psychology Today*, June 15, 2015, accessed June 26, 2019. https://www.psychologytoday.com/us/blog/where-science-meets-the-steps/201506/nature-s-antidepressant-the-dog.

CHAPTER 6

Professional Self-Care

*Choose a job you love and
you will never have to
work a day in your life.*
—Confucius
(Goodreads.com)

Most of us spend a large proportion of our time and energy in the workplace. According to the American Institute of Stress, occupational pressures and fears are the leading source of stress for American adults and it has continued to escalate in the past few years. The major causes are 46 percent workload, 28 percent people issues, 20 percent juggling work/personal lives, and 6 percent lack of job security. They recommend preventing stress with self-care including proper sleep, diet, exercise, avoidance of caffeine/stimulants, and taking time to relax.[32]

Several professional self-care strategies will be discussed in this chapter. It is important to weave nourishing and stress-relieving activities into your workday as you are able or feel the need. The chief

---

[32] "Workplace Stress," American Institute of Stress, June 26, 2019, https://www.stress.org/workplace-stress.

complaint that people who attend my stress-management workshops consistently share is difficulty maintaining balance between their work and personal lives. It is helpful to have letting-go strategies that assist you in leaving work at work and shifting focus toward your personal life at the end of the workday.

Seek and Maintain Supportive Professional Relationships

Having healthy, supportive relationships within the workplace can make work more enjoyable. It is encouraged to seek and maintain connections with positive peers, role models, supervisors, and coworkers. No one is going to understand the pressures of your work situation the way people who work within the organization or business do. Having enjoyable lunches, brainstorming sessions, a drink after work, or other occasional outings can be great ways to develop and maintain the bonds. When things are rough, we can seek help and support from these allies.

Take Breaks to Rejuvenate

Taking breaks is helpful to avoid physical, mental, and emotional exhaustion. Awareness, self-permission, and planning may be necessary to getting the respite you need. As humans, our bodies and minds need time for rest and rejuvenation to function optimally. It is essential to allow yourself to take breaks throughout the day, week, and year. While this may seem obvious, many people push themselves beyond what is healthy and do not take the time necessary to replenish.

Having a strong connection with your body, which is an amazing storehouse of information, is helpful as it will signal you when it is time to step away from the pressures of life. Intuiting messages from your body requires paying attention to how it feels. For example, if you are at work and notice tension in your shoulders and a sense of being overwhelmed, it would be a good time to leave your office and step outside for a few minutes. If you feel more tired than usual, you may want to take a nap or allow for extra sleep at night until you become revitalized. I encourage mindfulness regarding how you feel because it can provide information regarding what you need. Ignoring the body's signs can often lead to more serious situations, such as illness.

Breaks from work, responsibilities at home, and from life's pressures can have benefits such as improved health and wellness, reduced stress, shift in perspective, mental clarity, and increased productivity. Although taking a pause is an investment of time, the benefits and efficiency gained are worth finding the outlet.

Giving yourself permission to take a break is often necessary as it may seem as though there are not enough moments in the day to accomplish all that needs to be done. This can be especially important if the idea of taking a break makes you feel guilty, lazy, or unproductive. Repeating an affirmation in your mind, such as "It is okay for me to rest," might be helpful if you struggle with stepping away.

A lunch break is a great time to refresh and release stress of the morning by stepping away from your desk. People often work through the day with the notion that it will increase their productivity. You may, in actuality, find that you return with more clarity and energy, which can result in elevated efficiency. In addition to nourishing your body, you may create the space for a workout, enjoy being outdoors, or run an errand that would allow you to enjoy other evening activities. A luncheon with a coworker or friend can be a wonderful opportunity to have fun and develop supportive relationships. If taking breaks is not encouraged at your workplace, taking them each day anyway may be an opportunity to model effective self-care. An improved attitude and higher productivity would certainly have everyone wondering what your secret is!

Taking a pause, in the moment when you need it, is advisable but not always practical. I encourage you to find some time each day to rest and do something nurturing for yourself. This may require some planning or can be done spontaneously when you see a window of time. Good questions to ask yourself each day are "What breaks did I allow myself today?" and/or "What did I do for myself today?" You will gain awareness regarding your habits through answering these questions daily. From this place of understanding, you can make the necessary changes to accommodate your needs for rejuvenation.

Scheduling for rest and enjoyment each week is a good habit. Setting aside a large portion of time or a day of leisure can help you refresh and maintain balance. Additionally, taking vacation each year can be restorative, aid in maintenance of a positive outlook, and prevent burnout. Scheduled time off can be beneficial whether you go on a trip or stay home. Allowing yourself opportunities to do what you feel like doing in the moment can feel liberating and help release tension.

Taking breaks daily, weekly, and yearly is good self-care practice. Meeting your needs for rest, rejuvenation, and fun can help improve job satisfaction, prevent burnout, and result in a better quality of life.

Self-Care Strategies for Use While at Work

Breath Work

A great way to begin your day is by practicing breath work, as discussed in chapter 4. This can easily be done periodically throughout the day during brief breaks, while working independently, in meetings, when talking with clients, etc. to induce the parasympathetic relaxation response. No one will notice that you are breathing while you are working because you do it anyway! If you are in a profession that would support teaching self-care, like mental health, in the medical field, as a first responder, etc., you can begin appointments by facilitating breathing exercises with your clients or patients.

Mindfulness

If you are in a caregiving profession, as mentioned above, you may begin appointments with mindfulness by inviting your client or patient to slow down and observe his/her thoughts, physical body sensations, emotions, and behaviors in that moment, without judgment. Awareness can be gained through mindfulness and can be the springboard for a productive session. This is also a great way to get centered and maintain balance.

Keep a Yoga Mat in Your Office

When you need a time out, you can do gentle stretching or try one of these poses for relaxation and revitalization:

- Corpse pose—Lie on your back with limbs spread. Focus on your breath, allowing your abdomen to rise on the inhale and fall on the exhale. Set the intention of releasing any negative energy from your body as you breathe.
- Legs up the wall—Lie on your back with your bottom in the corner, where the wall meets the floor, and with your legs extended up the wall. Breathe and relax. This pose is great for energy circulation and replenishment.

Maintain Dual Focus

As discussed in a previous chapter, maintain a dual focus by continually paying attention to what is going on within yourself while engaging with other people and activities. Having a mindful inner focus can foster self-awareness, and it can be a reminder not to take on the stress and emotions of others.

Alter Your Work Environment

It can be a nice change in environment to work outside on a nice day. Open the windows to get fresh air, or work from home as appropriate and approved. Sometimes having a meeting or engaging in a project somewhere besides your office space can provide a shift in perspective necessary and break up monotony. Examples include working in a conference room, in someone else's office, or off-site at a coffee shop or restaurant.

Create a Calming Workspace

A soothing and peaceful work environment can help ease tension for yourself and others. This may not be appropriate in all workplace settings, but here are a few ideas. You may decorate your workspace with inspirational arts, quotes, sculptures, etc. to keep yourself inspired. Playing peaceful music or nature sounds such as waterfall, rain, ocean waves, or birds chirping softly in the background is very nurturing. If acceptable, use an oil diffuser with calming essential oils, such as rose, lavender, chamomile, or a blend designed for peace, relaxation, etc. (more on this in chapter 8). Sip on chamomile tea or a blend designed for relaxation while you work.

Set Clear and Healthy Boundaries

It is recommended that you set clear and healthy boundaries and limits while in the workplace. For example, end sessions and meetings on time so you do not get behind, communicate the time you need to leave at the end of the day, don't overcommit. As I mentioned before, sometimes we have to say no to others in order to say yes to ourselves. If we do not set and honor our boundaries, it's easy to get taken advantage of.

Organizational Skills and Time Management

If you struggle with organizational skills and time management, it is advisable to spend some time planning each day. Create to-do lists that are reasonable and prioritize. Remember that things usually take longer than we expect, and if we are overzealous by creating an unachievable list, we can become frustrated and disillusioned. Be realistic regarding what you can and cannot get done. Delegate whenever and wherever appropriate. It is also helpful to organize your workspace periodically to keep it clutter-free and functional. You will be more likely to think clearly by doing so. If you are not able to get this done during the workday, periodically spending a few hours on the weekend may be worth the time to help make you more effective during work hours.

Create a "Smile" File

It is important to find ways to remember and celebrate the joys and successes of your work. I encourage you to keep an electronic "smile file" and a paper "smile file" in your file cabinet. It is nice to have places to keep reminders of the meaningful times and successes at work. It can be helpful to look at these on the days when we feel challenged and less than adequate at work. Some examples of what you may want to keep in a smile file include cards from clients, positive letters or emails, awards, uplifting reviews, pictures, articles, etc. Anything that reminds you of fun times, your accomplishments, and achievements is advisable.

Letting-Go Strategies for Use Following Work

Many people struggle with taking their work home with them rather than leaving it at work. Incorporating letting-go strategies can assist in creating a boundary between professional and home life. Time away from the office is often more flexible and is an excellent time for self-care. Doing something to release stress and replenish yourself daily is encouraged to maintain the resiliency necessary to maintain balance. Try some of the ideas below or come up with some of your own letting-go strategies.

- Come up with an affirmation that helps you to release the day and say it as you leave the office. For example, "I've done my best, and I release the workday. Now it is time to enjoy my personal time."
- Roll the windows down as you leave work and let the fresh air cleanse your energy.
- Identify a letting-go song to play each day as you leave work, which signals that it is time to relax, play, etc.
- Read the serenity prayer.

- Swing by the park before you go home.
- Change into your comfy clothes right when you get home.
- Go outside for a walk, run, or bike ride.
- Take a sea salt or Epsom salt bath to unwind when you get home (relaxes muscles and cleanses your energy field).
- Meditate to clear the slate.
- Join a yoga or Pilates class that meets right after work as mind-body exercise can be a powerful release.
- Journal—express and release your emotions, set intentions and goals.
- Spend quality time with family, friends, and/or pets.
- Go to a movie or watch a favorite show.
- Do nothing.
- Read a magazine or book.
- Do breath work to induce the parasympathetic relaxation response.
- Spend time in nature—gardening, bird-watching, visiting the park or nature center, or whatever you enjoy doing outside.

I encourage you to find opportunities to laugh, have fun, play, and relax during time spent away from work in order to recharge and return to work refreshed. It is too easy to get caught in the demands and responsibilities of both work and the home/family. There will always be more to do, and sometimes it can wait. Your needs are important too! You will have more to give when you acknowledge and respond to your personal requirements.

Engaging the Spirit in Corporate Wellness

This section may be of particular use for people in leadership or influential roles within their organization. I share here a blog that I wrote in 2017 as it does pertain to professional self-care and corporate wellness.

The leadership of corporate wellness programs needs to adopt a holistic approach as they consider wellness options for their employees. An integrated strategy engages and develops the whole employee and celebrates the multidimensionality of each person. Physical, mental, emotional, spiritual components are ideally woven into a program to fully benefit the employees and the organization.

The spiritual component may seem surprising to many as something to include in corporate wellness, but let us be honest; we don't leave our spirit at home when we go to work. According to Google definitions, "The *spirit* is 'the nonphysical part of a person that is of emotion and character, the soul.'" To do so would be like coming to work incomplete and missing the part that makes us most unique. Stressful environments can erode the soul, drawing us further and further away from who we are at the core. We are at our personal best when we integrate and connect to our multidimensionality. In doing so, we have all our aspects available to us, including intellect, creativity, passion, emotion, intuition, logic, natural flow, and beyond. An organization with spirited employees is a healthy, thriving, and productive organization.

Stress is on the rise in many workplaces, as humans experience so many changes and job uncertainty. Incorporating mindfulness and stress-management education in corporate wellness is beneficial to the employees, clients, and the company. We must look at our organizations holistically and that includes incorporating the wellness of the employees. Offering informational and inspirational wellness workshops that invigorate the mind, relax the body, and feed the spirit are necessary in this day and age.

Valuing employees, those individuals who spend a great deal of their lives dedicated to the success and advancement of the business, is beneficial to everyone involved. Results may include employee satisfaction, improved employee health and well-being, better customer service, increased productivity, decreased absenteeism, and better interstaff relations. Sure, there is a cost for holistic workshops, but employees are worth investing in.

I recently *unplugged* by spending a few days in solitude at a yoga ashram in the mountains of Colorado. One day while I was visiting there was an organization that arranged a full-day retreat for its employees. I was surprised to be alongside corporate staff who were doing yoga, meditating, eating nutritious food, and hiking together. I spent part of my day observing and engaging with them. It was most impressive to see what this outing was doing. The reason I visited the ashram was to rejuvenate, gain clarity, and renew my spirit. Of course, this adventure both educated and renewed the spirits of these employees. It was simply brilliant, and I thought about how much experiences like these could potentially benefit every aspect of a business and its personnel.

In 2010, I taught Introduction to Mindfulness Meditation at a dozen social-service agencies in Wichita, Kansas. At the time, very few understood or had experienced mindfulness meditation. It was truly refreshing to employees as they opened to the new experience. I have been offering stress-management workshops that incorporate mindfulness meditation to professional caregivers and business professional for several years now. There has been an increasing openness and interest in incorporating this highly effective stress-reduction method into the lives of the people I instruct. In 2010, it seemed very progressive and somewhat "out there" for many people. In just a few years, it has become acceptable and mainstream.

We need a paradigm shift in which we include corporate wellness as an important aspect of the business model. This shift creates a sound, whole firm as we invest in the wholeness of the individuals working for the organization. Everyone benefits from a supportive work environment that encourages and invests in employee wellness.

Summary

With workplace stress on the rise, it is more important than ever to incorporate effective self-care methods into the workday. We must make taking care of our needs a priority if we are to maintain resiliency and longevity within our professions. This can be done by paying attention to the signals from the body and mindfully meeting its needs. These can be met through simple relaxation techniques incorporated into the day or done following work on a regular basis. These may include breath work, mindfulness, meditation, stretching, taking breaks to rejuvenate, eating lunch, creating a calming work environment, setting and maintaining clear and healthy boundaries, practicing good organization and time-management skills, noticing and appreciating the joys of your work, and incorporating letting-go strategies to leave work at work. By acknowledging and honoring your needs, you are likely to be more effective and feel better on all levels. Taking care of yourself is likely to benefit you, your clients or patients, your employer, and everyone you interact with. In some organizations this may be a paradigm shift, but you can lead by example by modeling effective self-care and demonstrating the benefits both personally and professionally.

The next chapter includes an overview of secondary trauma and special considerations for professional caregivers. This is a must-read for those in the medical and mental health fields, first responders, veterinary and shelter staff, educators, and others in professional caregiving roles. If the content does not apply or is not of interest to you, proceed to chapter 8, "Spiritual Self-Care."

CHAPTER 7

Secondary Trauma and Considerations for Professional Caregivers

A generous heart, kind speech, and a life of service and compassion are the things which renew humanity.
—**Buddha** (Azquotes.com)

Comprehensive self-care practices are especially essential for professional caregivers due to the high demand and intensity of their work. Caregivers in the medical and mental health fields, first responders, animal caregivers, educators, and others serve people who are often struggling or suffering with continuous empathy. They can be selfless in their dedication to serve others and are often left feeling depleted over time when their needs have not been adequately met. This can take a physical, mental, emotional, and spiritual toll on caregivers who are not counterbalancing the intensity with proactive and thorough care for themselves. There is a reason they are often considered *unsung heroes*. They show up and risk their lives during the most difficult situations humanity could possibly experience.

Many zealously enter their professions with an unwavering desire to help others and lose passion due to the deleterious effects of the work. Studies have demonstrated that professional caregivers are at high risk of experiencing secondary trauma—including, compassion fatigue, secondary traumatic stress, vicarious traumatization, and burnout.

Secondary trauma symptoms can come on gradually or suddenly following exposure to the trauma of another or others. It can be traumatic to witness the pain and suffering of others, especially for highly empathic individuals. Observing others going through struggles can trigger painful sensations and memories from the subconscious of the caregiver assisting. This indirect exposure to graphic material can be through hearing the stories told by clients/patients or by assisting them during or immediately following a trauma, such as during a life-threatening emergency or in the emergency room. If left unresolved, this can cause problems for the professional that build over time. The secondary traumatic stress injuries are similar and are often used interchangeably, yet have some differences as discussed below.

Secondary Stress Injuries

Compassion Fatigue

Charles Figley coined the term *compassion fatigue* in 1995 while doing a research study with nurses who did not like the stigma associated with the term *secondary traumatic stress*. Compassion fatigue relates to the emotional and physical exhaustion that can impact professional caregivers over time. It has been correlated with gradual desensitization to client/patient stories, a decrease in the quality of care provided by the caregiver, an increase in clinical errors, and rise of depression and anxiety among caregivers. This can result in increased stress leave and lack of concern and integrity in the workplace. Compassion fatigue often affects the caregiver's personal relationships by decreasing ability to connect with family and friends, which can lead to higher stress in households, divorce, and social isolation. The compassion and empathy that led the caregiver into service becomes diminished and difficult to access.[33]

Secondary Traumatic Stress

Secondary traumatic stress (STS) is a designation that refers to individuals who have become traumatized by hearing about an event experienced by a client or patient rather than through personal or direct experience. This can occur in the context of familial, societal, or through a professional relationship. The symptoms experienced are very similar to those described with posttraumatic stress disorder (PTSD) such as intrusive imagery, avoidance of reminders of an event, hypervigilance, distressing emotions, and compromised functioning. Severe instances of secondary traumatic stress may fit into the diagnosis of PTSD.[34]

Vicarious Traumatization

This term refers to trauma that causes a negative transformation in the psyche of the caregiver in the areas of thoughts, beliefs, worldview, and disruptions in spirituality leading to loss of hope and meaning in life. These alterations can be permanent if not treated effectively.[35]

Burnout

Burnout occurs when an individual experiences high stress with intensity over time. This can be a mixture of exhaustion with depression and anxiety. Lack of motivation can lead to low self-esteem, negative attitude, reduced effectiveness, and efficiency. Exposure

---

[33] Charles R. Figley, *Counterbalance the Intensity of Your Work: Compassion Stress Management Participant Workbook* (Tallahassee: Figley Institute), 4.

[34] Charles R. Figley, *Counterbalance the Intensity of Your Work: Compassion Stress Management Participant Workbook* (Tallahassee: Figley Institute), 4.

[35] Charles R. Figley, *Counterbalance the Intensity of Your Work: Compassion Stress Management Participant Workbook* (Tallahassee: Figley Institute), 4.

to trauma, fear, uncertainty, lack of financial security, and frustration over lack of control over circumstances can lead to burnout.[36] Professional caregivers are at high risk of burnout, although individuals can experience burnout within any position or responsibility. For example, people with corporate careers, monotonous and repetitive jobs, caretakers of foster children, parents of their children can also experience burnout. When a person experiences burnout within their role or profession, a change may be necessary because the individual often no longer enjoys his/her job. This could involve taking a vacation, a leave of absence, a shift in responsibilities, or a job change depending on the severity of the symptoms.

Compassion Fatigue—Warning Signs and Symptoms[37]

- Feeling estranged from others
- Difficulty falling or staying asleep
- Outbursts of anger or irritability with little provocation
- Startling easily
- While working with a victim thinking about violence or retribution against the perpetrator or person victimized
- Experiencing intrusive thoughts or flashbacks of interactions with difficult clients /patients or families
- Feeling there is no one to talk with about highly stressful experiences
- Working too hard for your own good
- Frightened of things traumatized people and their families have said or done to you
- Experiencing troubling dreams similar to a client/patient or their family

---

36 Charles R. Figley, *Counterbalance the Intensity of Your Work: Compassion Stress Management Participant Workbook* (Tallahassee: Figley Institute), 5.

37 Angelea Panos, "Understanding and Preventing Compassion Fatigue—A Handout for Professionals," retrieved July 24, 2020 from Gift from Within—PTSD Resources for Survivors and Caregivers, July 25, 2007, accessed June 24, 2019. http://www.giftfromwithin.org/html/prvntcf.html.

- Suddenly and involuntarily recalling a frightening experience while working with a client or patient
- Preoccupied with a client/patient or their family
- Losing sleep over a client/patient and their family's traumatic experiences
- Felt a sense of hopelessness associated with working with clients/patients and their families
- Have felt weak, tired, rundown as a result of your work as a caregiver
- Have felt depressed or trapped due to your work as a caregiver
- Unsuccessful at or finding it difficult to separate work life from personal life
- Feeling little compassion toward most of your coworkers
- Having thoughts that you are not succeeding at achieving your life goals
- Feeling that you are working more for the money than for personal fulfillment
- Having a sense of worthlessness / disillusionment / resentment associated with your work

There are a variety of conditions and factors that put professional caregivers at high risk of experiencing secondary trauma injuries. If you are in the field, you will likely be able to recognize or identify with the risk factors mentioned below for yourself, your workplace, or other workplaces within your discipline. They are self-explanatory and many have been discussed in detail previously in this book within the professional self-care chapter. The purpose of outlining risk factors here is to bring awareness that they exist and that is important to adopt self-care practices that counterbalance the inherent downfalls of working within the caregiving professions.

Risk Factors

- Continuous use of empathy and compassion
- Chronic exposure to other's traumatic events
- Repression of emotions

- Previous direct exposure to trauma
- Inability to control work stress
- Low compensation / high caseloads
- Work bureaucratic environment
- Inadequate supervisor support and training
- Lack of social support
- Underdeveloped coping / stress-management skills
- Putting others' needs above personal needs
- Unrealistic, self-imposed, and hard-to-meet expectations

Risk Factors according to Dr. Anna Baranowski, CEO of Traumatology Institute[38]

- Best and brightest in their field
- Those who expect positive feedback and outcomes
- Place high personal demand on self
- Low self-compassion
- Toleration of exhaustion
- Experiences of personal trauma
- Large and complex workload
- Lack of trauma training
- Overidentification with victims
- Workplace / family / friends are not supportive

---

[38] Baranowski, Anna B., "Compassion Fatigue Specialist (Therapist) Course." Accessed February 25, 2015. Htpps://www.ticlearn.com

Secondary Traumatic Stress Scale[39]

The following is a list of statements made by persons who have been impacted by their work with traumatized clients. Read each statement then indicate how frequently the statement was true for you in the past **seven (7) days** by circling the corresponding number next to the statement.

NOTE: "Client" is used to indicate persons with whom you have been engaged in a helping relationship. You may substitute another noun that better represents your work such as consumer, patient, recipient, etc. Copyright 1999 Brian E. Bride.

	0	1	2	3	4
	Never	Rarely	Occasionally	Often	Very Often
1. I felt emotionally numb					
2. My heart started pounding when I thought about my work with clients					
3. It seemed as if I was reliving the trauma(s) experienced by my client(s)					
4. I had trouble sleeping					
5. I felt discouraged about the future					
6. Reminders of my work with clients upset me					
7. I had little interest in being around others					
8. I felt jumpy					
9. I was less active than usual.					
10. I thought about my work with clients when I didn't intend to					
11. I had trouble concentrating					
12. I avoided people, places, or things that reminded me of my work with clients					
13. I had disturbing dreams about my work with clients					
14. I wanted to avoid working with some clients					
15. I was easily annoyed					
16. I expected something bad to happen					
17. I noticed gaps in my memory about client sessions					

---

[39] Charles R. Figley, *Counterbalance the Intensity of Your Work: Compassion Stress Management Participant Workbook* (Tallahassee: Figley Institute), 30.

Scoring Instructions[40]

For each subscale below, add your scores for the items listed. Add the three scores in the right-hand column for a total score.

Subscale	Items	Score
Intrusion	2 3 6 10 13	
Avoidance	1 5 7 9 12 14 17	
Arousal	4 8 11 15 16	
Total		

Scoring Instructions[41]

Little or No STS	Mild STS	Moderate STS	High STS	Severe STS
27 or less	28–37	38–43	44–48	49+

Get further testing for PTSD that is caused by STS.

---

[40] Charles R. Figley, *Counterbalance the Intensity of Your Work: Compassion Stress Management Participant Workbook* (Tallahassee: Figley Institute), 31.

[41] Charles R. Figley, *Counterbalance the Intensity of Your Work: Compassion Stress Management Participant Workbook* (Tallahassee: Figley Institute), 31.

Further testing for PTSD that is caused by STS is recommended if the following combination is present:

Intrusion	at least 1 item +
Avoidance	3 items +
Arousal	2 items

Caregiver Reactions and Impact of Professional Functioning

There are numerous ways that we can react while experiencing secondary trauma. These fall into the categories of cognitive, emotional, behavioral, spiritual, interpersonal, and physical reactions. An individual experiencing secondary trauma can exhibit a few or a variety of the following reactions in one or more categories outlined in the following chart. The impact of secondary trauma encountered by the helper can make it difficult to meet the expectations of the job adequately. The negative impact on professional functioning can be noted in the areas of performance of job tasks, morale, interpersonal deficiencies, and behavioral tendencies. The chart on the next page outlines the undesirable impact/effects.[42]

Healthy Coping Strategies

A variety of healthy coping strategies have been mentioned throughout the book that can counterbalance the impact of secondary stress. The upcoming chart outlines healthy coping strategies in the categories of cognitive, emotional, behavioral, spiritual, interpersonal, and physical for quick reference. Incorporating these strategies and others which have been discussed are helpful since self-care has been identified through research as the greatest way to reduce or prevent secondary trauma in the professional caregiver. Everything you do for yourself, big or small, can make a difference moving toward recovery, rejuvenation, and/or prevention.

---

[42] Charles R. Figley, *Counterbalance the Intensity of Your Work: Compassion Stress Management Participant Workbook* (Tallahassee: Figley Institute), 38–39.

Caregiver Reactions[43]

Table 1: Caregiver Reactions		
Cognitive	**Emotional**	**Behavioral**
o Diminished concentration	o Powerlessness	o Clingy
o Confusion	o Anxiety	o Impatient
o Spaciness	o Guilt	o Irritable
o Loss of meaning	o Anger/rage	o Withdrawn
o Decreased self-esteem	o Survivor guilt	o Moody
o Preoccupation with trauma	o Shutdown	o Regression
	o Numbness	o Sleep disturbances
o Trauma imagery	o Fear	o Appetite changes
o Apathy	o Helplessness	o Nightmares
o Rigidity	o Sadness	o Hypervigilance
o Disorientation	o Depression	o Elevated startle response
o Whirling thoughts	o Hypersensitivity	o Use of negative coping (smoking, alcohol or other substance abuse)
o Thoughts of self-harm or harm toward others	o Emotional roller coaster	
	o Overwhelmed	
o Self-doubt	o Depleted	o Accident proneness
o Perfectionism		o Losing things
o Minimization		o Self harm behaviors
Spiritual	**Interpersonal**	**Physical**
o Questioning the meaning of life	o Withdrawn	o Shock
	o Decreased interest in intimacy or sex	o Sweating
o Loss of purpose		o Rapid heartbeat
o Lack of self-satisfaction	o Mistrust	o Breathing difficulties
o Pervasive hopelessness	o Isolation from friends	o Aches and pains
o Ennui	o Impact on parenting (protectiveness, concern about aggression)	o Dizziness
o Anger at God		o Impaired immune system
o Questioning of prior religious beliefs	o Projection of anger or blame	
	o Intolerance	
	o Loneliness	

[43] Charles R. Figley, *Counterbalance the Intensity of Your Work: Compassion Stress Management Participant Workbook* (Tallahassee: Figley Institute), 38–39.

Impact on Professional Functioning			
Performance of Job Tasks	Morale	Interpersonal	Behavioral
o Decrease in quality o Decrease in quantity o Low motivation o Avoidance of job tasks o Increase in mis-takes o Setting perfectionist standards o Obsession about details	o Decrease in confidence o Loss of interest o Dissatisfaction o Negative attitude o Apathy o Demoralization o Lack of appreciation o Detachment o Feelings of incompleteness	o Withdrawal from colleagues o Impatience o Decrease in quality of relationship o Poor communication o Subsume own needs o Staff conflicts	o Absenteeism o Exhaustion o Faulty judgment o Irritability o Tardiness o Irresponsibility o Overwork o Frequent job changes

Table 2: Healthy Coping Strategies[44]

Cognitive	Emotional	Behavioral
o Moderation	o Moderation	o Moderation
o Write things down	o Allow yourself to experience what you feel	o Spend time by yourself
o Make small, daily decisions	o Label what you are experiencing	o Spend time with others
o See the decisions you are already making	o Give yourself permission to ask for help	o Limit demands on time and energy
o Giver yourself permission to ask for help	o Be assertive when necessary	o Help others with tasks
o Plan for the future	o Keep communication open with others	o Give yourself permission to ask for help
o Get the most information you can to help make decisions	o Remember you have options	o Do activities that you previously enjoyed
o Anticipate needs	o Use your sense of humor	o Take different routes to work or on trips
o Remember you have options	o Have a buddy with whom you can vent	o Remember you have options
o Review previous successes	o Use "positive" words and language	o Find new activities that are enjoyable and (mildly) challenging
o Problem solve	o Practice, Practice, Practice	o Set goals, have a plan
o Have a Plan "B"		o Relax
o Break large tasks into smaller ones		o Practice, Practice, Practice
o Practice, Practice, Practice		

---

[44] Charles R. Figley, *Counterbalance the Intensity of Your Work: Compassion Stress Management Participant Workbook* (Tallahassee: Figley Institute), 38–39.

Spiritual	Interpersonal	Physical
o Moderation	o Moderation	o Moderation
o Discuss changed beliefs with spiritual leader	o Give yourself permission to ask for help	o Aerobic exercise
o Meditation	o Take time to enjoy time with trusted friend/ partner	o See doctor and dentist
o Give yourself permission to ask for help		o Routine sleep patterns
o Practice rituals of your faith/beliefs	o Hugs	o Minimize caffeine, alcohol, and sugar
o Spiritual retreats/ workshops	o Healthy boundaries	o Give yourself permission to ask for help
o Prayer	o Remember to use "I" statements	o Eat well-balanced, regular meals
o Remember you have options	o Use humor to diffuse tense conversations	o Drink water
o Mindfulness	o Play together	o Wear comfortable clothes
o Find spiritual support	o Talk with trusted partner/ friend	o Engage in physical luxuries: spa, massage, bath, personal trainer
o Read Spiritual literature	o Apologize when stress causes irritable behavior or outbursts	o Remember to breathe – deeply
o Practice, Practice, Practice	o State needs and wants as clearly as possible	o Take mini breaks
		o Practice, Practice, Practice

Compassion Satisfaction

Dr. Beth Hudnall Stamm stated that the "Compassion satisfaction is the pleasure we derive from being able to do our work well. Higher levels of compassion satisfaction are related to the ability to be an effective caregiver."[45] The Professional Quality of Life Scale (ProQOL) version 5 (2009) was developed by Stamm and can be

---

[45] Charles R. Figley, *Counterbalance the Intensity of Your Work: Compassion Stress Management Participant Workbook* (Tallassee: Figley Institute), 27–29.

used to measure compassion satisfaction, burnout, and secondary traumatic stress.[46] This self-assessment is available on the next page.

There are multiple ways in which compassion satisfaction can be cultivated. Rather than focusing on the negative or challenging aspects of the work, one can generate positive feelings by appreciating the aspects of the work that are enjoyable. Remembering accomplishments, positive feedback from clients/patients/supervisors, times when a difference was made in someone's life, and feeling gratitude for such opportunities can help shift our perspective and elevate our mood. Creation of a "smile file" to keep positive feedback from others, awards, cards, etc. can be helpful to review at times when the work seems overwhelming and you have lost sight of your positive impact.

Building a support network within the workplace can make work more enjoyable. Reaching out to people in the same profession for support is helpful as they are likely to have experienced similar frustrations and joys while doing their jobs. It is nice to take time out to enjoy lunch and conversations with friends at work. Identifying supervisors and mentors to whom you can go for advice and/or learning opportunities can be gratifying.

Effective self-care can help you maintain resiliency and keep your balance, thus contributing to compassion satisfaction. Creating balance between work, family/friends, and personal needs is essential. Continually assessing and adjusting self-care between these three areas is important in establishing and maintaining balance. When it seems as if one area of your life is dominating the others, it is time to make an adjustment. To do so requires contemplation and mindfulness regarding what is working and what is not.

I encourage you to find opportunities to laugh, have fun, play, and relax during time spent away from work in order to recharge and return to work refreshed. It is too easy to get caught up in the demands and responsibilities of both work and the home/family.

---

[46] Charles R. Figley, *Counterbalance the Intensity of Your Work: Compassion Stress Management Participant Workbook* (Tallassee: Figley Institute), 27–29. Permission granted by ProQOl office, The Center for Victims of Torture. https://proQOL.org. ProQOL measure is available for free in many languages at www.ProQOL.org.

There will always be more to do, and sometimes it can wait. Your needs are important too! You will be more effective and have more to give when you acknowledge and respond to your needs.

Professional Quality of Life Scale[47]

Symptoms of compassion fatigue can appear gradually or suddenly depending on the individual's circumstances. The ProQOL version 5 was developed to measure compassion satisfaction, burnout, and secondary traumatic stress (compassion fatigue). The self-assessment is provided here and is a valuable tool to take periodically to gauge where you are at with the measures.

When you *[help]* people you have direct contact with their lives. As you may have found, your compassion for those you *[help]* can affect you in positive and negative ways. Below are some questions about your experiences, both positive and negative, as a *[helper]*. Consider each of the following questions about you and your current work situation. Select the number that honestly reflects how frequently you experienced these things in the *last 30 days*.

1 = Never   2 = Rarely   3 = Sometimes   4 = Often   5 = Very Often

1. I am happy.
2. I am preoccupied with more than one person I *[help]*.
3. I get satisfaction from being able to *[help]* people.
4. I feel connected to others.
5. I jump or am startled by unexpected sounds.
6. I feel invigorated after working with those I *[help]*.
7. I find it difficult to separate my personal life from my life as a *[helper]*.

---

[47] Charles R. Figley, *Counterbalance the Intensity of Your Work: Compassion Stress Management Participant Workbook* (Tallassee: Figley Institute), 27–29. Permission granted by ProQOl office, The Center for Victims of Torture. https://proQOL.org. ProQOL measure is available for free in many languages at www.ProQOL.org.

8. I am not as productive at work because I am losing sleep over traumatic experiences of a person I *[help]*.
9. I think that I might have been affected by the traumatic stress of those I *[help]*.
10. I feel trapped by my job as a *[helper]*.
11. Because of my *[helping]*, I have felt "on edge" about various things.
12. I like my work as a *[helper]*.
13. I feel depressed because of the traumatic experiences of the people I *[help]*.
14. I feel as though I am experiencing the trauma of someone I have *[helped]*.
15. I have beliefs that sustain me.
16. I am pleased with how I am able to keep up with *[helping]* techniques and protocols.
17. I am the person I always wanted to be.
18. My work makes me feel satisfied.
19. I feel worn out because of my work as a *[helper]*.
20. I have happy thoughts and feelings about those I *[help]* and how I could help them.
21. I feel overwhelmed because my case [work] load seems endless.
22. I believe I can make a difference through my work.
23. I avoid certain activities or situations because they remind me of frightening experiences of the people I *[help]*.
24. I am proud of what I can do to *[help]*.
25. As a result of my *[helping]*, I have intrusive, frightening thoughts.
26. I feel "bogged down" by the system.
27. I have thoughts that I am a "success" as a *[helper]*.
28. I can't recall important parts of my work with trauma victims.
29. I am a very caring person.
30. I am happy that I chose to do this work.

© B. Hudnall Stamm, 2009. *Professional Quality of Life: Compassion Satisfaction and Fatigue Version 5 (ProQOL)*. www.isu.edu/~bhstamm or www.proqol.org. This test may be freely copied as long as (a) author is credited, (b) no changes are made, and (c) it is not sold.

Your Scores on the ProQOL: Professional Quality of Life Screening

Based on your responses, place your personal scores below. *If you have any concerns, you should discuss them with a physical or mental health-care professional.*

Compassion Satisfaction_____

Compassion satisfaction is about the pleasure you derive from being able to do your work well. For example, you may feel like it is a pleasure to help others through your work. You may feel positively about your colleagues or your ability to contribute to the work setting or even the greater good of society. Higher scores on this scale represent a greater satisfaction related to your ability to be an effective caregiver in your job.

The average score is 50 (SD 10; alpha scale reliability .88). About 25% of people score higher than 57 and about 25% of people score below 43. If you are in the higher range, you probably derive a good deal of professional satisfaction from your position. If your scores are below 40, you may either find problems with your job, or there may be some other reason—for example, you might derive your satisfaction from activities other than your job.

Burnout_____

Most people have an intuitive idea of what burnout is. From the research perspective, burnout is one of the elements of Compassion Fatigue (CF). It is associated with feelings of hopelessness and difficulties in dealing with work or in doing your job effectively. These negative feelings usually have a gradual onset. They can reflect the feeling that your efforts make no difference, or they can be associated with a very high workload or a non-supportive work environment. Higher scores on this scale mean that you are at higher risk for burnout.

140

The average score on the burnout scale is 50 (SD 10; alpha scale reliability .75). About 25% of people score above 57 and about 25% of people score below 43. If your score is below 43, this probably reflects positive feelings about your ability to be effective in your work. If you score above 57 you may wish to think about what at work makes you feel like you are not effective in your position. Your score may reflect your mood; perhaps you were having a "bad day" or are in need of some time off. If the high score persists or if it is reflective of other worries, it may be a cause for concern.

Secondary Traumatic Stress_____

The second component of Compassion Fatigue (CF) is secondary traumatic stress (STS). It is about your work related, secondary exposure to extremely or traumatically stressful events. Developing problems due to exposure to other's trauma is somewhat rare but does happen to many people who care for those who have experienced extremely or traumatically stressful events. For example, you may repeatedly hear stories about the traumatic things that happen to other people, commonly called Vicarious Traumatization. If your work puts you directly in the path of danger, for example, field work in a war or area of civil violence, this is not secondary exposure; your exposure is primary. However, if you are exposed to others' traumatic events as a result of your work, for example, as a therapist or an emergency worker, this is secondary exposure. The symptoms of STS are usually rapid in onset and associated with a particular event. They may include being afraid, having difficulty sleeping, having images of the upsetting event pop into your mind, or avoiding things that remind you of the event.

The average score on this scale is 50 (SD 10; alpha scale reliability .81). About 25% of people score below 43 and about 25% of people score above 57. If your score is above 57, you may want to take some time to think about what at work may be frightening to you or if there is some other reason for the elevated score. While higher scores do not mean that you do have a problem, they are an indication that you may want to examine how you feel about your work and your work environment. You may wish to discuss this with your supervisor, a colleague, or a health care professional.

What Is My Score and What Does it Mean?

In this section, you will score your test so you understand the interpretation for you. To find your score on each section, total the questions listed on the left and then find your score in the table on the right of the section.

Compassion Satisfaction Scale

Copy your rating on each of these questions on to this table and add them up. When you have added then up, you can find your score on the table to the right.

3. ___
6. ___
12. ___
16. ___
18. ___
20. ___
22. ___
24. ___
27. ___
30. ___
Total: ___

The sum of my Compassion Satisfaction questions is	And my Compassion Satisfaction level is
22 or less	Low
Between 23 and 41	Moderate
42 or more	High

Burnout Scale

On the burnout scale, you will need to take an extra step. Starred items are "reverse scored." If you scored the item 1, write a 5 beside it. The reason we ask you to reverse the scores is because, scientifically, the measure works better when these questions are asked in a positive way though they can tell us more about their negative form. For example, question 1. "I am happy" tells us more about the effects of helping when you are not happy, so you reverse the score.

*1. ___ = ___
*4. ___ = ___
8. ___
10. ___
*15. ___ = ___
*17. ___ = ___
19. ___
21. ___
26. ___
*29. ___ = ___
Total: ___

You Wrote	Change to
	5
2	4
3	3
4	2
5	1

The sum of my Secondary Trauma questions is	And my Secondary Trauma Stress level is
22 or less	Low
Between 23 and 41	Moderate
42 or more	High

Secondary Traumatic Stress Scale

Just like you did on Compassion Satisfaction, copy your rating on each of these questions on to this table and add them up. When you have added then up, you can find your score on the table to the right.

2. ___
5. ___
7. ___
9. ___
11. ___
13. ___
14. ___
23. ___
25. ___
28. ___
Total: ___

The sum of my Burnout questions is	And my Burnout level is
22 or less	Low
Between 23 and 41	Moderate
42 or more	High

Ethics of Self-Care

Caregivers tend to be so focused on helping others that many do not often dedicate enough time and resources for their personal care. Some feel guilty or selfish when their focus is turned toward themselves. Self-care for the caregiver should be viewed as a professional ethical obligation and not as an option. When a caregiver is not adequately taking care of his/her needs, it can put the client/patient at risk. Good self-care practices can help the caregiver to perform the responsibilities of his/her position optimally and with increased compassion.

Most professional codes of ethics include statements regarding *impairment* and some address caregiver *self-care* more directly. The Green Cross Academy of Traumatology has comprehensive standards of self-care guidelines that are designed for professional caregivers. This code states that the purpose of the guidelines is twofold: "First, do no harm to yourself in the line of duty when helping/treating others. Second, attend to your physical, social, emotional, and spiritual needs as a way of ensuring high-quality services to those who look to you for support as a human being."[48]

Most codes of ethics begin with the principle of "first, do not harm," as it relates to the client/patient. While this is a must, it is also imperative that we maintain a dual focus on the client/patient and ourselves while doing our caregiving work to ensure optimal service, to uphold the integrity of our professions, and to maintain personal well-being. Ethical errors are more likely to occur when the caregiver experiences symptoms of compassion fatigue and/or burnout. Self-care has been identified as the greatest protection against experiencing secondary trauma symptoms because it increases caregiver resiliency.

Compassion fatigue is linked to ethical errors; therefore, it stands to reason that it is unethical to neglect self-care. Self-care is the responsibility of each professional. The benefits of practicing effective self-care are far reaching and can impact everyone you interact with. Self-care is ethical practice!

---

[48] Charles R. Figley, *Counterbalance the Intensity of Your Work: Compassion Stress Management Participant Workbook* (Tallassee: Figley Institute), 7.

Green Cross Academy of Traumatology is the organization through which I earned certifications as a compassion fatigue therapist and compassion fatigue educator. In my prior research regarding various codes of ethics inclusion of self-care standards, I found Green Cross has the most comprehensive and clear guidelines. Green Cross Academy of Traumatology is an international nonprofit humanitarian assistance organization comprised of trained traumatologists and compassion-fatigue service providers. More information regarding Green Cross can be found at www.greencross.org. See below for their standards of self-care.

Green Cross Academy of Traumatology Standards of Self-Care[49]

I. Purpose of the Guidelines

As with the standards of practice in any field, the practitioner is required to abide by standards of self-care. These Guidelines are utilized by all members of the Green Cross. The purpose of the Guidelines is twofold: **First, do no harm to yourself** in the line of duty when helping/treating others. Second, attend to your physical, social, emotional, and spiritual needs as a way of ensuring high quality services to those who look to you for support as a human being.

II. Ethical Principles of Self-Care in Practice

These principles declare that it is unethical not to attend to your self-care as a practitioner because sufficient self-care prevents harming those we serve.

---

[49] Staff Green Cross Academy of Traumatology, "Standards of Care," accessed July 24, 2020, https://greencross.org/about-gc/standards-of-care-guidelines.

1. **Respect for the dignity and worth of self**: A violation lowers your integrity and trust.
2. **Responsibility of self-care**: Ultimately it is your responsibility to take care of yourself and no situation or person can justify neglecting it.
3. **Self-care and duty to perform**: There must be a recognition that the duty to perform as a helper cannot be fulfilled if there is not, at the same time, a duty to self-care.

III. Standards of Humane Practice of Self-Care

1. **Universal right to wellness:** Every helper, regardless of her or his role or employer, has right to wellness associated with self-care.
2. **Physical rest and nourishment:** Every helper deserves restful sleep and physical separation from work that sustains them in their work role.
3. **Emotional rest and nourishment:** Every helper deserves emotional and spiritual renewal both in and outside the work context.
4. **Sustenance modulation:** Every helper must utilize self-restraint with regard to what and how much they consume (e.g., food, drink, drugs, stimulation) since it can compromise their competence as a helper.

IV. Standards for Expecting Appreciation and Compensation

1. **Seek, find, and remember appreciation from supervisors and clients:** These and other activities increase worker satisfactions that sustain them emotionally and spiritually in their helping.

2. **Make it known that you wish to be recognized for your service:** Recognition also increases worker satisfactions that sustain them.
3. **Select one or more advocates:** They are colleagues who know you as a person and as a helper and are committed to monitoring your efforts at self-care.

V. Standards for Establishing and Maintaining Wellness

Section A. Commitment to self-care

1. **Make a formal, tangible commitment:** Written, public, specific, and measurable promise of self-care.
2. **Set deadlines and goals:** the self-care plan should set deadlines and goals connected to specific activities of self-care.
3. **Generate strategies that work and follow them:** Such a plan must be attainable and followed with great commitment and monitored by advocates of your self-care.

Section B: Strategies for letting go of work

1. **Make a formal, tangible commitment:** Written, public, specific, and measurable promise of letting go of work in off hours and embracing rejuvenation activities that are fun, stimulating, inspiriting, and generate joy of life.
2. **Set deadlines and goals:** The letting go of work plan should set deadlines and goals connected to specific activities of self-care.

3. **Generate strategies that work and follow them:** Such a plan must be attainable and followed with great commitment and monitored by advocates of your self-care.

Section C. Strategies for gaining a sense of self-care achievement

1. **Strategies for acquiring adequate rest and relaxation:** The strategies are tailored to your own interest and abilities which result in rest and relaxation most of the time.
2. **Strategies for practicing effective daily stress reductions method(s):** The strategies are tailored to your own interest and abilities in effectively managing your stress during working hours and off-hours with the recognition that they will probably be different strategies.

VI. Inventory of Self-care Practice—Personal

Section A: Physical

1. **Body work:** Effectively monitoring all parts of your body for tension and utilizing techniques that reduce or eliminate such tensions.
2. **Effective sleep induction and maintenance:** An array of healthy methods that induce sleep and a return to sleep under a wide variety of circumstances including stimulation of noise, smells, and light.
3. **Effective methods for assuring proper nutrition:** Effectively monitoring all food and drink intake and lack of intake with the

awareness of their implications for health and functioning.

Section B: Psychological

1. **Effective behaviors and practices to sustain balance between work and play**
2. **Effective relaxation time and methods**
3. **Frequent contact with nature or other calming stimuli**
4. **Effective methods of creative expression**
5. **Effective skills for ongoing self-care**
   a. **Assertiveness**
   b. **Stress reduction**
   c. **Interpersonal communication**
   d. **Cognitive restructuring**
   e. **Time management**
6. **Effective skill and competence in meditation or spiritual practice that is calming**
7. **Effective methods of self-assessment and self-awareness**

Section C: Social/interpersonal

1. **Social supports:** At least five people, including at least two at work who will be highly supportive when called upon
2. **Getting help:** Knowing when and how to secure help—both informal and professional—and the help will be delivered quickly and effectively
3. **Social activism:** Being involved in addressing or preventing social injustice that results in a better world and a sense of satisfaction for trying to make it so

VII. Inventory of Self-Care Practice— Professional

1. **Balance between work and home:** Devoting sufficient time and attention to both without compromising either
2. **Boundaries/limit setting:** Making a commitment and sticking to regarding
   a. Time boundaries/overworking
   b. Therapeutic/professional boundaries
   c. Personal boundaries
   d. Dealing with multiple roles (both social and professional)
   e. Realism in differentiating between things one can change and accepting the others
3. **Getting support/help at work through:** Making a commitment and sticking to it regarding
   a. Peer support
   b. Supervision/consultation/therapy
   c. Role models/mentors
4. **Generating Work Satisfaction:** By noticing and remembering the joys and achievements of the work

VIII. Prevention Plan Development

1. **Review current self-care and prevention functioning.**
2. **Select one goal from each category.**
3. **Analyze the resources for and analyze the resistances to achieving goal.**
4. **Discuss goal and implementation plan with support person.**
5. **Activate plan.**

6. **Evaluate plan weekly, monthly, yearly with support person.**
7. **Notice and appreciate the changes.**

The Preventative Benefits of Self-Care

The benefits of self-care are numerous for both the individual caregiver and the organization. We need to move away from the model of "self-less" service and lean into "self-full" services. That is, providing services from the full use of one's self. This paradigm shift will be increasingly necessary as we are seeing drastic changes on the rise. The individual who commits to comprehensive and effective self-care benefits through the experience of improved health, optimized energy, reduced stress, life balance, better relationships, and an improved quality of life. This benefits the organization through improved delivery of services, increased production, reduction of errors, reduced turnover, decreased absences, and better inter-staff relations.

Addressing Self-Care at Multiple Levels

What we need is a self-care movement in which each person loves, cares, and takes responsibility for one's self. By acknowledging and responding to our needs, we have more energy and compassion for those we serve. As professional caregivers, we have the influence to greatly impact our clients/patients by teaching and modeling effective self-care. We have the opportunity to create and lead a self-care movement, but in order to do so, we must be proficient with our personal self-care and *walk our talk*. It begins right here, within us and our professions.

Several researchers of secondary trauma related to caregiving professionals have identified self-care as an issue that should be addressed within multiple levels. This is important due to the high-risk caregivers face of experiencing stress injuries due to the intense nature of their work and exposure to secondary trauma. Self-care should be viewed as the responsibility of the individual, of educators in the academic setting, and at the professional level within the workplace.

The individual can address self-care by holding himself/herself to a high standard of self-care practice. By maintaining a commitment to excellent self-care habits, the caregiver is more likely to maintain balance and resilience during times of occupational stress. It is helpful to design a self-care plan that has specific intentions regarding self-care methods and frequency of application (see page 214). The individual caregiver can seek out self-care resources and tools through research, training workshops, online training, and working with qualified professionals. Additionally, working toward wholeness within ourselves by healing unresolved issues and traumas can be liberating.

Self-care can be addressed within academia by including stress management and self-care courses into the university's curriculum. An ideal time to offer such courses is when students are doing on-the-job practicums and internships. Creating awareness regarding secondary trauma and teaching effective stress-management tools before entering the caregiving professions could better prepare students to handle the intensity of their work and result in career longevity.

Organizations can address self-care by providing their employees with stress management/self-care training and continuing education. Wellness programs are an excellent way to support employees with their self-care needs. The organization can reinforce professional self-care by encouraging employees to take lunch breaks, providing manageable workloads and reasonable work hours, ensuring adequate supervision and training, and cultivating a positive environment that results in employee satisfaction.

By addressing self-care within multiple levels, caregivers are more likely to experience satisfaction and flourish within their work. When the caregiver is feeling optimal, he/she can provide superior client/patient care. From this place, the caregiver can positively impact the client/patient by modeling and teaching effective self-care. This is an opportunity to create much needed change within our society.

*Be the change that
you wish to see
in the world.*
—Ghandi
(Goodreads.com)

Summary

There are special considerations that should ideally be taken into account as a professional caregiver in the fields of medical and mental health, veterinary and animal services, first response, education, and similar fields. Having awareness regarding increased risk of experiencing secondary stress injuries such as compassion fatigue, secondary traumatic stress, vicarious traumatization, and burnout in these professions is important. Understanding and identifying the warning signs and symptoms, risk factors, adverse professional functioning and reactions within oneself and others can help prevent or resolve instances of secondary stress through appropriate self-care.

Self-care has been identified as the greatest prevention and remedy for secondary stress injuries. The ideal is that professionals in caregiving professions can stay connected to the joys of their work and experience compassion satisfaction, the opposite of compassion fatigue. Self-care is an ethical practice to honor the needs of both the caregiver and the clients/patients they serve through high-quality care. The ideal is that self-care is addressed at multiple dimensions including by the individual caregiver, in academic and professional settings to increase satisfaction, high service standards, and career longevity.

CHAPTER 8

Spiritual Self-Care

Happiness cannot be traveled to, owned, earned, worn or consumed. Happiness is the spiritual experience of living every minute with love, grace and gratitude.
—**Dennis Waitley,** American motivational speaker, writer, and consultant (Brainyquote.com)

For those deeply spiritual people, our spirituality is woven into the fabric of our being. It is an inseparable aspect when we recognize ourselves as spiritual beings having a physical experience and knowing that our souls are eternal. Spiritual self-care is to the soul like water is to a plant. It feeds our spirit and nurtures our soul. It is uplifting and essential. When we disconnect from our spiritual practices and beliefs, it is like falling off the path into a ditch and getting back on the path feels like coming home.

For those who do not currently engage in spiritual practices or spiritual self-care, it is something worth considering. Spirituality is very personal, and some consider themselves to be spiritual, independent of religion. How these individuals find meaning in life is a subjective experience and includes psychological growth independent of a religious context. For some, their spiritual path infuses spirituality and religion through a shared system of beliefs, faith, and worship.

I am deeply spiritual but not affiliated with a particular religion. I continually experience a connection with God, the Universe, Source, and all that is. The psychological inner work I have done has opened me to become a clear channel for Divine energies to work through. My experience includes connection with archangels, angels, ascended masters, spirit guides, and spirit healers.

My spiritual self-care consists of use of my intention, prayer, and simple practices throughout the day to clear my energy and to maintain a conscious clear connection with source energy and my spirit helpers. It also includes reading spiritual literature and attending spiritual workshops that assist me in a continuous growth and unfolding process.

Commitment to my path of service is also source of spiritual practice, as I get to teach other like-minded and like-hearted individuals through my workshops. In my world, it is all connected and it's all spirit—spirit in service of spirit, whether in human or nonhuman form. My life is infused with love in every aspect. It began with learning to love every aspect of myself and understanding that I am an aspect of God, as is everyone and everything. Then it expanded to include love for all of humanity and an experience of *oneness* of all that is.

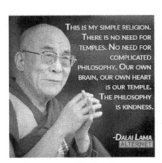

Figure 2. Dalai Lama Spread Love #82: This is my simple religion (jeremychin.com)

As I speak of spirituality in this chapter, I am not trying to tell or convince anyone of what they should believe. Your beliefs and practices are yours—yours to explore and experience. You will know if they resonate with your soul based on how you feel inside. Do your beliefs and practices help you feel supported, empowered, free, safe, uplifted, expanded, and inspired? Do they leave you feeling fearful, unworthy, shameful, or guilty? These things are worth considering as I've worked with many people who have adopted the religious beliefs and practices ingrained in them as children who later, following careful introspection and inner work, discovered that what they were taught does not resonate with their soul.

I encourage you to question everything and keep only that which resonates with you. This advice can be applied within every area within your life, including your spiritual beliefs and affiliations. This questioning can be uncomfortable and lead to a lot of letting go, which can also be very freeing.

Reexamine all you've been told...Dismiss what insults your soul.
—**Walt Whitman**
(Goodreads.com)

Mindfulness and Meditation

The concepts of mindfulness have been discussed several times in this book and have been intertwined throughout. Some people use meditation and mindfulness to relax and help relieve stress, but they can be taken much further when infused within our spiritual practices.

Meditation can serve to help us connect deeply within ourselves to help us access more of what is available within us. It can be used as a tool to connect with God, Source, the Creator, the Universe, or whatever is your chosen term for the Source from which everything exists. We can deeply connect with our spirit helpers, ascended masters, angels, or whatever your spiritual and/or religious beliefs include. It can help us sense the *oneness* of all humanity and of everything that is. We can connect with and sense the inner light within ourselves through deep meditation. Meditation can be a time of deep introspection and contemplation in which the answers to our questions can arise from deep within us or though connection with Divine beings. Our infinite potential can be accessed and explored through this practice.

Meditation is infused within many spiritual practices. I have had several religious people question meditation as if it is "out there" or too "new age." According to the Bible, Jesus meditated. Prayer can be considered a meditation. If you have been reluctant to meditate for religious reasons, you might explore and see for yourself how it can be included into your spiritual self-care.

Here is a testimonial that someone sent me following a mindfulness-meditation retreat that I led a few years ago through my business Blossoming Heart Center. I include it to demonstrate how a religious person who was once not open to meditation chose to explore it and found it to be a pleasant experience. This person, who I choose to keep anonymous for the sake of her privacy, decided to attend my weekly meditations, which helped her to heal from the loss of her husband and stay centered while raising their four children as a widow. She even brought a few of her older children to some meditations to help them cope with their grief.

> Having come from a Religious Christian background, I was taught meditation was bad. However, in my own studies I came across a scripture that said to "meditate on it, day and night," (Joshua 1:8). Then I saw that Isaac in Genesis 24:63 went out to meditate. Not to mention that we are supposed to "take captive every thought and imagination," (2 Corinthians 10:5). I went on a Christian prayer retreat and found that *prayer* was the Christian word for meditation. So I ventured to my first group meditation workshop with Suzie. I was pleasantly surprised! It was the most relaxation that I had experienced in over a year since I'd lost my husband, and there was absolutely nothing to fear. I was told before we even started what to expect and given the

freedom to make my own decisions if something didn't feel right without offending her. I freely participated in the whole event and left feeling refreshed, energetic, and knew I would return again."—Anonymous client

Practice Rituals of Your Faith and Beliefs

Rituals have been around since the early recordings of humankind within religious and spiritual sects. These include sequences, repetitive acts, and ceremonies that are meaningful within a person's religious or spiritual practices. The engagement in these is considered powerful and sacred. I will not go into the details of any specific rituals, as I do not know all of them. Rituals can help you connect with yourself, your spirit helpers, God, and other high vibrational spirits. Their purposes can be to cleanse and purify, uplift, celebrate, pray, heal, and beyond. Rituals have specific intentions, which can make them powerful.

The purpose of mentioning rituals is not to educate you but to remind you that if rituals are an important aspect of your faith and beliefs, they can be included in your spiritual self-care. Rituals do not have to be prescribed by someone else. There may be some ritual you create that help you with your spiritual connection and self-care.

Spiritual Retreats and Workshops

Attending spiritual retreats or workshops can be an amazing way to uplift and feed the soul. Sometimes we need to get out of the daily grind of our routines and into a different environment for exploration, introspection, and growth to occur. Spiritual retreats and workshops often include spiritually astute teachers who have traveled interesting spiritual paths and have much to share to help others heal and grow. Spending time with like-minded and like-hearted people while exploring studies and exercises. around your spiritual interests can be nourishing, heart-centering, and expansive.

Spiritual retreats can be short and done within a day or a few days. They can involve travel, overnight stays, and longer periods of time in more of an immersion setting. Workshops can be shorter (an hour or a few hours), local, and easy to incorporate within your regular schedule. These may also be more along the line of a retreat, extensive, and involve travel (or not). Your purpose can be simply to relax and rejuvenate or to go deeper within your inner landscape.

If you are spiritually oriented or want to explore spirituality, I highly encourage retreats and/or workshops as a form of spiritual self-care. Many of these are now available online.

Prayer

When we pray, we can ask for help, request support, express gratitude, and connect and communicate with a higher power than ourselves that aligns with our belief system. This may be very comforting and help us feel safe in a world that can be unsettling at times. It is nice to know that we are never alone and that we can always call upon our Divine, whoever and whatever that is, for personal assistance and love. We can pray for our own help and well-being or for our loved ones and others in need of assistance. Our prayers can be personal or include meaningful shared prayers such as the Lord's Prayer and the Knights Templar Prayer.

Many people speak of the power of prayer and have witnessed or experienced unexplainable occurrences following, which could be considered miracles. Sometimes it is obvious that a power beyond our intellect has intervened and changed the course for our or someone else's life. These *miracles* can be small, everyday miracles or larger and life-changing. There are even studies that have been done to demonstrate how prayer has been successful in the felt sense of well-being and brought about healing phenomena.

Many churches and spiritual gatherings include a prayer box in which attendees can include written requests for prayers for themselves and others. Following a service or event, the designated person or people pray for the person/people who need assistance.

Some people engage in prayer groups that include many people gathering to pray together, with the idea that there is power in num-

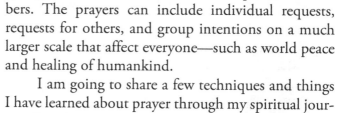

bers. The prayers can include individual requests, requests for others, and group intentions on a much larger scale that affect everyone—such as world peace and healing of humankind.

I am going to share a few techniques and things I have learned about prayer through my spiritual journey. I am by no means trying to convince you to pray or tell you how to pray. These are merely possibilities, and you are free to choose whether or not they resonate with you.

Another way to pray is to use the Vesica Pisces symbol (see to the right) in conjunction with written prayers to distance yourself from the situation and turn it over to a higher power. I learned this technique at a Healing Miracles Workshop with Rev./Dr. Michael Ulm and Rev./Dr. Ellen Valentine-Laperriere through All Light Ministries. The idea is that when you are immersed in a problem, you are in reaction mode rather than response mode. The sacred geometry symbol of Vesica Pisces can be used to separate yourself or another from the problem by placing God between the person and the issue. This allows the highest good for everyone involved to become a reality.

Figure 3. Vesica Pisces, the Healing Miracles Workshop

The significant problems we have cannot be solved at the same level of thinking with which we created them.
—Albert Einstein
(Quotes.net)

This means we need to request that a higher consciousness intervene to solve the problem. This can be done by including God and higher consciousness such as Jesus, Buddha, Mother Mary, etc. in the prayer request. To use the Vesica Pisces symbol, you would write your name or the person you are praying for at the bottom and write the problem or problem person's name at the top. The center area is where God/Jesus/Spirit/Christ Consciousness/Buddha Consciousness/ or whatever higher power is within your belief system resides.[50]

The prayer can also be done with the Tri-Vesica Pisces symbol by placing the desired intention or outcome of the prayer in the center of the symbol. The three circles represent the power of three elements for spiritual balance and unity, which stands for different things in different cultures.

Examples include

- Mind, body, spirit;
- Air, water, earth;
- Mother, Father, child;
- Father, Son, Holy Spirit;
- Past, present, future.

I recently showed a few clients how to use the Vesica Pisces symbol for prayer, and they got amazing results. One gentleman had an employer that had promised him a bonus and was overdue. He scheduled a meeting with the leadership to express his frustration. He did the prayer a day before the meeting. The meeting went well; they cut him a check for $20,000 that day and made a commitment to start talking about elevating his career path.

I have another client who has done the inner work necessary to let go of her former partner(s), beliefs, and patterns within herself that set her up to attract unhealthy romantic relationships. She recently did the Vesica Pisces prayer with the intention of attracting her ideal romantic partner at the right and perfect time. A week later, she was out with a friend, who suggested they go to an unusual place for their girls' night out. She met a romantic interest who was unlike

---

[50] Michael L. Ulm and Ellen R. Valentine-Laperriere, *All Light Ministries Healing Miracles Workshop Manual* (Charlotte: All Light Ministries, 2018), 42.

anyone she had ever dated yet seems to possess the ideal qualities to be a long-term romantic partner. Their relationship is progressing beautifully, and they are discussing marriage.

I have a prayer box in which I write my prayers on tiny pieces of paper with the Vesica Pisces symbol. I put the prayers into the box and intend that they are done. It is a way that I can put my intentions out there and trust that they are being heard and taken care of by God. Sometimes I bless my prayer box by channeling Divine love through my hands. You can simply do this by connecting with your Divine and intending that Divine love flow through your crown chakra (energy center located at the top of your head), down through your head, neck, shoulders, arms, and through your hands. It is much like the way I do hands-on healing through my healing practice. It's really not me that blesses it or does the work; I am simply a vessel through which it can flow where directed.

Things to consider when praying are as follows:

- Instead of attaching or intending a certain outcome while praying, intend or ask that whatever is in the highest and best good for everyone involved is done. We don't always know, from our limited human perspectives, what is in the highest and best good for ourselves or others.
- It's also helpful to pray that things are done according to Divine will and in Divine right order or timing.
- And be sure to include gratitude as if it is already done.
- This can be taken further by feeling the sensation of what it will be like when the prayer has come to reality. Feeling the relief, joy, excitement, etc. as if it is already here can be very powerful.
- If you choose to be specific with the prayer, you might include the phrase *or better* following your intentions.[51]

I would like to share a personal example of a prayer someone else was doing on my behalf (that I recently learned about through

[51] Michael L. Ulm and Ellen R. Valentine-Laperriere, *All Light Ministries Healing Miracles Workshop Manual*, (Charlotte: All Light Ministries, 2018), 131–136.

my sister-in-law). During the time in which I was separated from my former husband, my brother was praying for us to stay together. His intentions were pure as he was praying for what he thought was best for our family, based on his understanding of our situation and his beliefs about marriage. Praying for whatever is in someone's highest and best good takes your ideas, beliefs, perceptions, preferences out of the prayer and makes it more open to all the possibilities, including what is best for the person.

My sister-in-law shared this with me recently, after over eleven years of divorce. I am glad his prayer did not come true, as I am happier than ever. I believe that it was perfect that my former husband and I came together to have many experiences and three beautiful children and that it is perfect that we chose to go down our separate paths to have experiences more aligned with the evolution of our souls. The children have done well with the divorce and are thriving. It seems that the contrast between two very different households and parenting styles has made them adaptable, resilient, and more open to differences. I cannot say that it has always been easy, but it has kept all of us growing.

Seek Spiritual Support

It is helpful to stay in connection with like-hearted and like-minded spiritual people who understand and care about you. Your spiritual support network can include a romantic partner, family, friends, mentors, groups, church leaders, spiritual counselors, and other people you trust. These people often have a shared sense of meaning and such relationships can have an indescribable depth.

These can be people you can turn to during difficult times for support, perspective, and inspiration. But I would not wait until everything goes wrong to reach out. It is nice to maintain these relationships, and they can be some of the best that you'll ever have.

And be sure to seek spiritual support through your nonhuman helpers on a regular basis through prayer, meditation, and intended connection. These ongoing relations can help carry you through your days and make life much better. Another benefit is that your nonhuman spiritual support is always available to help, 24-7 and 365 days a year.

Read Spiritual Literature

We can participate in spiritual self-care through reading spiritual literature. This can include books, magazines, blogs, and other high vibrational works. You know what type of writings most resonates with your spiritual beliefs. For one person, this could be the Bible; for another, it could be the Koran; for someone else, it may be *The Power of Now* by Eckhart Tolle; and for another, it may be the *Four Agreements: A Practical Guide to Personal Freedom* by Don Miguel Ruiz. There are so many forms of spiritual literature available, and only you can decide what is best for you. These literary works can be uplifting and remind us to stay true to our values and beliefs. Reading books is a great way to explore spirituality if you are unsure of which direction to go.

Connect with Nature

Spending time outdoors connecting with nature can be an amazing experience of oneness with all that is. After all, we too are part of the natural world, so spending time in nature helps us to connect more deeply within ourselves and realize that we are not separate from existence. It is an opportunity to engage our senses by smelling the aromas present, hearing the sounds around us, enjoying the beautiful sights, feeling the textures around, and the emotions within. The experiences to be found on Mother Earth are limitless and can include breathing fresh air, connecting with animals, birds, flowers, trees, bathing in the sun, gazing at the stars and moon, watching the clouds pass by, and beyond.

Time spent outdoors can be nurturing, grounding, and revitalizing. It can help clear the mind, reduce stress, invoke positive emotions, and ground us within our bodies and our connection to the earth. Grounding, also referred to as earthing, has been shown to have physical benefits, such as reduced inflammation in the body.

Connecting with nature can be a truly spiritual experience as we witness spirit moving through everything and sense the spirit within ourselves. It can be awe-inspiring and freeing!

Spiritual Intelligence Self-Report Inventory (SISRI-24)[52]
© 2008 D. King

Below you will find a self-assessment and spiritual model regarding spiritual intelligence developed by David B. King as found in Figley Institute's *Counterbalance the Intensity of Your Work: Compassion Stress Management Workbook*. Although spirituality is very subjective, these tools are an interesting way to gauge spiritual awareness. These tools were obtained from the Figley Institute's *Counterbalance the Intensity of Your Work: Compassion Stress Management Workbook*.

The following statements are designed to measure various behaviors, thought processes, and mental characteristics. Read each statement carefully and choose which **one** of the five possible responses best reflects you by circling the corresponding number. If you are not sure, or if a statement does not seem to apply to you, choose the answer that seems the best. Please answer honestly and make responses based on how you actually are rather than how you would like to be. The five possible responses are:

0	1	2	3	4
Not at all true of me	Not very true of me	Somewhat true of me	Very true of me	Completely true of me

For each item, circle the **one** response that most accurately describes **you**.

1.	I have often questioned or pondered the nature of reality.	0	1	2	3	4
2.	I recognize aspects of myself that are deeper than my physical body.	0	1	2	3	4
3.	I have spent time contemplating the purpose or reason for my existence.	0	1	2	3	4

---

[52] Charles R. Figley, *Counterbalance the Intensity of Your Work: Compassion Stress Management Participant Workbook* (Tallassee: Figley Institute, 2013), 23–26.

4.	I am able to enter higher states of consciousness or awareness.	0	1	2	3	4
5.	I am able to deeply contemplate what happens after death.	0	1	2	3	4
6.	It is *difficult* for me to sense anything other than the physical and material.	0	1	2	3	4
7.	My ability to find meaning and purpose in life helps me adapt to stressful situations.	0	1	2	3	4
8.	I can control when I enter higher states of consciousness or awareness.	0	1	2	3	4
9.	I have developed my own theories about such things as life, death, reality, and existence.	0	1	2	3	4
10.	I am aware of a deeper connection between myself and other people.	0	1	2	3	4
11.	I am able to define a purpose or reason for my life.	0	1	2	3	4
12.	I am able to move freely between levels of consciousness or awareness.	0	1	2	3	4
13.	I frequently contemplate the meaning of events in my life.	0	1	2	3	4
14.	I define myself by my deeper, non-physical self.	0	1	2	3	4
15.	When I experience a failure, I am still able to find meaning in it.	0	1	2	3	4
16.	I often see issues and choices more clearly while in higher states of consciousness/awareness.	0	1	2	3	4
17.	I have often contemplated the relationship between human beings and the rest of the universe.	0	1	2	3	4

18. I am highly aware of the nonmaterial aspects of life.	0	1	2	3	4
19. I am able to make decisions according to my purpose in life.	0	1	2	3	4
20. I recognize qualities in people which are more meaningful than their body, personality, or emotions.	0	1	2	3	4
21. I have deeply contemplated whether or not there is some greater power or force (e.g., god, goddess, divine being, higher energy, etc.).	0	1	2	3	4
22. Recognizing the nonmaterial aspects of life helps me feel centered.	0	1	2	3	4
23. I am able to find meaning and purpose in my everyday experiences.	0	1	2	3	4
24. I have developed my own techniques for entering higher states of consciousness or awareness	0	1	2	3	4

Spiritual Intelligence Self-Report Inventory (SISRI-24) Scoring Procedures

Total Spiritual Intelligence Score:
Sum all item responses or subscale scores (after accounting for ***reverse-coded** item).

24 items in total; Range: 0–96

4 Factors/Subscales:

I. Critical Existential Thinking (CET): Sum items 1, 3, 5, 9, 13, 17, and 21.
7 items in total; range: 0–28

II. <u>Personal Meaning Production (PMP)</u>: Sum items 7, 11, 15, 19, and 23.
5 items in total; range: 0–20

III. <u>Transcendental Awareness (TA)</u>: Sum items 2, **6***, 10, 14, 18, 20, and 22.
7 items in total; range: 0–28

IV. <u>Conscious State Expansion (CSE)</u>: Sum items 4, 8, 12, 16, and 24.
5 items in total; range: 0–20

*Reverse Coding: Item # 6 (response must be reversed prior to summing scores).
Higher scores represent higher levels of spiritual intelligence and/or each capacity.

<u>Permissions for Use</u>

Use of the SISRI is unrestricted so long as it is for academic, educational, or research purposes. Unlimited duplication of this scale is allowed with full author acknowledgement only. Alterations and/or modifications of any kind are strictly prohibited without author permission.

The author would appreciate a summary of findings from any research which utilizes the SISRI.

Contact David King at dbking@live.ca

For additional information, please visit http://www.dbking. net/spiritualintelligence/ or e-mail

A Viable Model of Spiritual Intelligence[53]
(King, 2008; King & DeCicco, 2009)

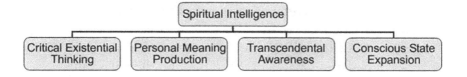

In the current model, **spiritual intelligence** is defined as a set of mental capacities which contribute to the awareness, integration, and adaptive application of the nonmaterial and transcendent aspects of one's existence, leading to such outcomes as deep existential reflection, enhancement of meaning, recognition of a transcendent self, and mastery of spiritual states.

An extensive literature review suggests four main components of spiritual intelligence:

I.   **Critical Existential Thinking**: the capacity to critically contemplate meaning, purpose, and other existential/metaphysical issues (e.g., existence, reality, death, the universe); to come to original existential conclusions or philosophies; and to contemplate non-existential issues in relation to one's existence (i.e., from an existential perspective).

II. **Personal Meaning Production**: the ability to derive personal meaning and purpose from all physical & mental experiences,

---

[53] Charles R. Figley, *Counterbalance the Intensity of Your Work: Compassion Stress Management Participant Workbook* (Tallassee: Figley Institute, 2013), 26.

including the capacity to create and master (i.e., live according to) a life purpose.

III. **Transcendental Awareness**: the capacity to identify transcendent dimensions/patterns of the self (i.e., a transpersonal or transcendent self), of others, and of the physical world (e.g., holism, nonmaterialism) during normal states of consciousness, accompanied by the capacity to identify their relationship to one's self and to the physical world.

IV. **Conscious State Expansion**: the ability to enter and exit higher/spiritual states of consciousness (e.g. pure consciousness, cosmic consciousness, unity, oneness) at one's own discretion (as in deep contemplation or reflection, meditation, prayer, etc.).

Spiritual intelligence performs quite well according to traditional criteria for intelligence. The above model satisfies the primary criterion: spiritual intelligence represents a set of mental abilities, as opposed to behaviors or experiences (click on each capacity for a detailed discussion).

For more detail, and for support according to additional criteria, read David's thesis on spiritual intelligence here: http://www.dbking.net/spiritualintelligence/2009ijts.pdf.

in any way is strictly prohibited. All information should be referenced as follows:

King, D. B. *Rethinking claims of spiritual intelligence: A definition, model, & measure.* Unpublished master's thesis, Trent University, Peterborough, Ontario, Canada (2008).

Summary

Spiritual self-care is essential for the spiritually attuned individual. It is an area worth exploring if you are desiring expansion, deeper connection with all that is, and discovering your Divine purpose on this earthly plane. This can be done through mindfulness and meditation, practicing rituals of your faith and beliefs, attending spiritual workshops and retreats, seeking like-minded and like-hearted spiritual support, reading spiritual literature and through connection with nature. Spirituality is deeply personal and varies by individual. Part of the spiritual path is discovering yourself and your personal truths. Much can be gained through spiritual self-care practices.

CHAPTER 9

Energy Management and Clearing

> *Everything is energy and that's all there*
> *is to it. Match the frequency of the reality*
> *you want and you cannot help but get*
> *that reality. It can be done no other way.*
> *This is not philosophy. This is physics.*
> **—Albert Einstein**
> (Awakenthegreatnesswithin.com)

Energy

Energy has been mentioned many times throughout this book. Some people consider energy to be a bit of a "woo-woo" or "out there" topic and prefer not to acknowledge that it exists, although the term *energy* is being used more freely and understood by many as an important part of reality. For people who are more sensitive, experiencing subtle energies within oneself and the external world is as natural as breathing. Although, not always easy.

This chapter may be particularly useful for people who are empathetic, highly sensitive, extremely open or going through a spiritual ascension process. People who are not empathic may not experience such difficulties with energy management. Additionally, individuals who maintain higher vibrations and connection with source energy on a steady and regular basis may not need as much help with energy management as their connection with source energy continually replenishes and protects against energies of lower vibration. If this is not of interest to you, simply discard it or skip to the next chapter.

Albert Einstein believed that everything is energy. Einstein's formula $E=MC^2$ (energy = matter) demonstrates this concept. All matter is an expression of energy, including our bodies, emotions, thoughts, and beliefs. Humans are comprised of subtle energies. Physical and emotional disturbances result from imbalances in energy. The proper flow and balance of life energies is essential for optimal health and well-being.

Subtle energy is also called life force, prana, chi, qi, and it is understood to flow though invisible energy pathways in the human body called meridians. There are seven main chakras in the human body known as energy centers that align up the spine, beginning at the pelvic floor and traveling up to the crown of the head. Chakras are shaped like discs that spin, where matter meets consciousness.

Michelle Fondlin, Vedic educator for the Chopra Center stated, "These swirling wheels of energy correspond to massive nerve centers in the body. Each of the seven main chakras contain bundles of nerves and major organs as well as our psychological, emotional, and spiritual states of being. Since everything is moving, it is essential that our seven main chakras stay open, aligned, and fluid. If there is a blockage, energy cannot flow. Think of something as simple as your bathtub drain. If you allow too much hair to go into the drain, the bathtub will back up with water, stagnate, and eventually bacteria and mold will grow. So is too with our bodies and the chakras."[54]

We can keep our chakras balanced through awareness, energy management, and proper self-care. This can be done through a variety of methods including the inner work previously discussed, acupuncture, yoga, acupressure, Reiki, tai chi, qi gong, applied kinesi-

---

[54] Michelle Fondlin, "What is a Chakra?" October 8, 2019, https://chopra.com/articles/what-is-a-chakra.

ology, meditation, and breath work. Additionally, there are personal energy-clearing practices you can do to keep your energy field free of energetic impurities and residues, which will be covered later in this chapter.

Energy Centers—Chakras

Below you will find basic information about the seven main chakras. If these are of interest to you, you can research each chakra in more depth. This information is simply to provide basic awareness. If you struggle with discomfort, pain, or health issues around one or more of your chakras, it is advisable to further investigate with a complimentary health provider who can provide some assistance with energetically clearing and balancing your chakras. This could in turn help with health issues and complement any medical treatment you currently seek for the issue.

The first three chakras are associated with the physical world, the world of matter. The fourth chakra is considered the bridge between matter and the spiritual world. The fifth through seventh chakras are chakras of higher consciousness and spirit.[55]

The first chakra is called the root chakra and is located at the base of the spine. If you were to meditate on this chakra, you would imagine it to be the color red. It is associated with safety, security, and basic needs. When this chakra is open, we feel safe, fearless, and as if our needs are being met. A person with a closed root chakra may experience difficulty grounding and pelvic pain, for example.[56]

The second chakra is called the sacral chakra and is located above the pubic bone and below the navel. The color affiliated to this chakra is orange. This chakra is associated with creative expression. It is also connected to sexuality, which is also relates to

[55] Michelle Fondlin, "What is a Chakra?" October 8, 2019, https://chopra.com/articles/what-is-a-chakra.

[56] Michelle Fondlin, "What is a Chakra?" October 8, 2019, https://chopra.com/articles/what-is-a-chakra.

0 which is related to creation. I have noticed the trend that victims of sexual abuse often need to work within this chakra to heal and open it. Not doing so can result in issues with the reproductive system.[57]

The third chakra is called the solar plexus chakra, which is found between the navel and breastbone. The color linked to this chakra is yellow. This chakra is also known as the power center since it is associated with our personal power. This chakra often requires opening when someone struggles with insecurity, lack of confidence, powerlessness, and lack of personal boundaries.[58]

The fourth chakra, known as the heart chakra, is housed in the center of the chest. The color corresponding with this chakra is green. The heart chakra bridges the lower three chakras, associated with matter, and the upper three chakras, which relate to higher consciousness and spirit. The heart is also considered to be a spiritual center. This chakra is considered the center of love and connection. It serves to connect body, mind, emotions, and spirit. Someone with a congested or blocked heart chakra may have difficulty feeling love, compassion, and connection with others. A variety of heart-related hurts such as loss, betrayal, and abandonment. could cause issues with this chakra.[59]

The fifth chakra is called the throat chakra, and someone who lives, speaks, and knows his/her personal truth will have an open throat chakra. The color linked with this chakra is blue. On the contrary, if someone has a blocked throat chakra, he/she may experience difficulty speaking personal truths, feel conflicted as if not living his/her personal truth, and experience physical issues such thyroid problems, throat pain, chronic cough, tickle in the throat, to name a few issues. I have worked with several clients who had thyroid dysfunc-

[57] Michelle Fondlin, "What is a Chakra?" October 8, 2019, https://chopra.com/articles/what-is-a-chakra.
[58] Michelle Fondlin, "What is a Chakra?" October 8, 2019, https://chopra.com/articles/what-is-a-chakra.
[59] Michelle Fondlin, "What is a Chakra?" October 8, 2019, https://chopra.com/articles/what-is-a-chakra.

tion that improved by doing the emotional healing necessary to live and speak their personal truths.[60]

The sixth chakra is also called the third eye. It is located at the center of the forehead and is known as the intuition center. The color associated with this chakra is indigo. A person with an open sixth chakra is connected to and listens to his/her personal intuition. Intuition is something that anyone can develop and learn to trust.[61]

The seventh chakra is known as the crown chakra, found at the crown of the head, and is affiliated with connection to the higher spiritual realms, higher consciousness, God, the Higher Self, the I Am presence, and to all that is. A person with an open crown chakra has done much work to open all the chakras beneath to reach the point of such connection with Source. This chakra is also associated with enlightenment. The color which corresponds to this chakra is violet.[62]

Aura

Another important concept to discuss as it pertains to energy and energy management is the aura. This is the protective energy field that surrounds the human body, and it can be weakened if you do not practice good self-care. The first line of defense is physical health. The second line of defense is emotional health, and the third line of defense is mental health. These all serve to maintain and strengthen your energy field. Energy management and clearing practices can help further nourish and clear the aura of negative energies and residues, keeping the aura healthy and vibrant.

---

[60] Michelle Fondlin, "What is a Chakra?" October 8, 2019, https://chopra.com/articles/what-is-a-chakra.

[61] Michelle Fondlin, "What is a Chakra?" October 8, 2019, https://chopra.com/articles/what-is-a-chakra.

[62] Michelle Fondlin, "What is a Chakra?" October 8, 2019, https://chopra.com/articles/what-is-a-chakra.

Empaths and Highly Sensitive People

Empaths are highly sensitive people who sense the emotions of others, as if they are their own. It can be difficult for an empath to distinguish what he or she is really feeling versus what they are picking up from other people. This occurs in varying degrees, depending on the extent to which one is empathic, as no two people experience the world the same. Many people are empaths and do not realize it. They often wonder why they are so emotional, feel drained after spending time with other people or in public, feel things so intensely, and/or become overstimulated easily.

According to Judith Orloff, MD, "Empaths have an extremely reactive neurological system. We do not have the same filters that other people do to block out stimulation. As a consequence, we absorb into our own bodies both the positive and stressful energies around us. We are so sensitive that it's like holding something in a hand that has fifty fingers instead of five. We are truly 'super responders.'"[63]

Orloff states "research shows that high sensitivity affects approximately 20 percent of the population, though the degree to one's sensitivity can vary. Empaths are often labeled as 'overly sensitive' and told to 'get a thicker skin.'"[64]

I happen to be one of those highly empathic people. I have always been empathic but did not understand this and found it difficult to deal with until the past several years when I began to understand my energetic experience and spiritual gifts. This is not uncommon for people who are highly sensitive or empathic. A good share of people who come to me as clients struggle with comprehension and management of their energetic boundaries when we begin the work. Or as they open through doing deep inner work, they must learn how to incorporate energy management into their self-care practices.

---

[63] Judith Orloff, *The Empath's Survival Guide* (Boulder: Sounds True Publishing, 2017), 2.

[64] Judith Orloff, *The Empath's Survival Guide* (Boulder: Sounds True Publishing, 2017), 2.

The human experience can be very difficult for empaths until they realize they are empathic and learn practices and strategies to more effectively deal with the challenges of this reality. There are many gifts that come with such sensitivity, but it can seem more like a curse until it is understood.

I have also noticed while doing presentations and training workshops for professional caregivers that many are empaths but do not realize it until I introduce the concept and characteristics. Being empathic as a caregiver is a great quality to have and is often helpful in the caregiving professions, yet few understand the personal vulnerability involved with being overly empathetic with clients and patients. This can lead to secondary trauma injuries such as compassion fatigue, secondary traumatic stress disorder, vicarious traumatization, and burnout.

Some signs that you could be an empath include the following:

- Highly sensitive
- Absorb other people's emotions
- Are introverted
- Highly intuitive
- Need a lot of time alone
- Can become overwhelmed in intimate relationships
- Targets for energy vampires
- Become replenished in nature
- Have finely tuned senses
- Have huge hearts, but sometimes give too much of themselves[65]

If you suspect that you are an empath, you may benefit from doing further research and reading about empaths. There are a few books that I recommend to many of my clients, which help them to further understand themselves and offer practices and strategies to help with energy management. These are *The Empath's Survival*

---

[65] Judith Orloff, *The Empath's Survival Guide* (Boulder: Sounds True Publishing, 2017), 34–35.

Guide: Life Strategies for Sensitive People by Judith Orloff and *The Highly Sensitive Person: How to Thrive When the World Overwhelms You* by Elaine Aron.

> *Everything changes when you start to emit your own frequency rather than absorbing the frequencies around you, when you start imprinting your intent on the Universe rather than receiving an imprint from existence.*
> —**Barbara Marciniak,** author, intuitive channel (Goodreads.com)

Energy Vampires

Energy vampires are people who are emotionally and energetically draining to be around. It is as if they siphon your energy and leave you feeling exhausted. Some people are more vulnerable to the negative effects of energy vampires than others, especially empaths. Many energy vampires are unaware that they drain energy, and then there are some who intentionally draw upon the energy of others. People who fall in this category are inclined toward codependency and are excessively emotionally and psychologically reliant on others. They have tendencies toward insecurity, narcissism, victim mentality, jealousy, negativity, etc. Such negativity can feel assaultive to a highly sensitive person.

It can be helpful to identify if there are people in your life who do this. If so, it is important to distance yourself or put up energetic and emotional boundaries, so they are not able to siphon your energy. This can be done by getting less personal with the individual, imagining yourself in a field of protective white, gold, pink, or blue light, or by keeping your distance. It is also recommended to do some inner work to help identify what is it about you that attracts this type of individual. For example, do you have codependent tendencies, overshare personal details of your life, get drawn into drama, and/or feel the need to help everyone you encounter? Examining your beliefs regarding your personal power can be most beneficial.

Strengthen Your Personal Power

We often do not understand, claim, or accept our personal power and thus give it away to others. This can leave us vulnerable to negative people and lower vibrational energies. A critical aspect to strengthening your energetic experience relates to understanding and connecting with your personal power. We have more energetic resiliency and sovereignty when we do the work within ourselves to access our personal strength and power. An important aspect of this is examining our beliefs regarding personal power. I often do subconscious-belief repatterning work with my clients regarding this topic. Here are some of the life-affirming beliefs that clients accept as their truth through doing the work.

- "I truly own and express my personal power."
- "I am sovereign over my own thoughts, emotions, and beliefs."
- "I have sovereignty over my energy at all times."
- "I am energetically sovereign and am unaffected by the energies of others."
- "My aura is healed, strong, and secure."
- "My aura is strong, and I am divinely protected at all times."
- "I am impervious to all negative and toxic energies."

Energy Grounding

Grounding is an important component of self-care and energy management. There are two important points to grounding—one being truly present in your body, and the other is feeling connection with the earth. Mindfulness helps one to be present and anchored within the body, as it fortifies the mind-body connection. Feeling embraced by the earth is also important. Experiencing both presence in the body and connection with the earth can help us feel calm and centered.

If you find yourself feeling spacey, unable to concentrate, engaged by an overactive mind, worried, stressed, or anxious, you would likely benefit from spending some time grounding and centering.

The earth's energy is of a higher vibration and can be very replenishing. We can tap into the energy of the earth to calm, center, balance, enhance, and strengthen our physical energy and energy field. It is very simple and can be done through spending time outdoors doing things such as walking barefoot in the grass, leaning up against a giant tree, sitting or standing on the ground, or doing anything outside in nature. It is even more powerful when we use our intention to connect with the earth as we are doing these things.

We can also ground by doing intentional exercises. This technique can be done indoors or outdoors. Imagine that you are a tree, with roots growing out of your feet into the earth. You can sense the energy and stability of the earth holding you in place. Then imagine the earth's energy coming up through those imaginary roots, up through your feet, up your legs, into your core, and eventually filling your entire body. Much like water nourishes a tree when it is watered, sustenance beginning at the roots, moving up the trunk, through the branches to the leaves. We can fill ourselves up much the same way through our intention. Once you sense you are filled up with the earth's energy, give yourself a few minutes to enjoy the new space that you have created within.

I incorporate a similar grounding exercise into most sessions with my clients, as they often feel much lighter following the release of emotional energies. As my clients sit before me, I ask them to imagine that their feet are very heavy and that they sink a few feet into the ground. I then invite them to connect with the energy of the earth beneath them and to draw the energy up through the entire body, starting with the feet; up through the ankles, the legs, the core; down the arms; and up to the top of the head. I also ask them to allow the energy to fill in any empty spaces from where they released emotional energy during the session. Additionally, I guide them to strengthen their aura through intention by utilizing the powerful earth energy. Simply feeling the earth's energy emanating around them, like being protected in a cocoon, accomplishes this. They leave feeling calm, balanced, centered, and whole. It helps them to adjust to the new space that they have created within themselves, which usually feels unfamiliar, that results from doing the healing and releasing work.

These exercises can be done anytime you need to calm yourself and stabilize. You can use your imagination to come up with grounding exercises that work for you or simply connect through your intention. In my case, the more grounded and open I've become, the easier it is to connect, and I can do it by simply saying, "Mother Earth, I'd like to connect with you now." Then I feel the rush of energy up through my feet and into my body. I feel grounded most of the time, but this is like an extra boost.

I connect and draw upon the earth's energy intentionally prior to each client session, going out in public, engaging in a difficult conversation, an important meeting, speaking in public, or when I am stressed or overly excited. It gives me the added energy I need to sustain myself. It also serves as an energetic protection to be grounded and filled up with higher vibrations from the earth. This energy is calming and soothing, which is especially helpful when you are around lower vibrations.

Scott Jeffrey has a great guide that explores the science and benefits of grounding and earthing. It also includes nine simple and effective grounding techniques and exercises. You can find these exercises at https://scottjeffrey.com/grounding-techniques/.

Create a High Vibrational Space

Another way that you can support and enhance your energy is by creating a high vibrational space, whether this is in your home, at the office, or both. Some people start with one room in the house that is designated as a calm, relaxing, or sacred space. The purpose of this room is often a place to meditate, contemplate, do yoga, or to retreat in privacy. Some make changes throughout the entire home to create a higher vibration to help with energetic support. There are a variety of ways to do this, which I will go into detail.

Open the Windows

A great way to raise the energetic frequency of your home is to open the windows. The free-flowing air of the outdoors can freshen up the indoors by allowing the pure energy of nature in. It also helps the clear stagnant energy and allows an escape for lower vibrational energies.

Cleanse and Purify Using Smudging Techniques

If you wish to take things a step further, you can open the windows in the house and energetically clear it by doing "smudging" of the house. The smudging ceremony is a Native American custom, also used by other indigenous cultures, to create a cleansing smoke bath to purify the body, aura, personal articles, and/or any space of negative energy. If you choose to try this, it is also important to be clear about your intention to cleanse and purify the space. Here are some simple smudging instructions for clearing a space:

- Open the windows prior to beginning, to allow for heavy and dense energies to be released outside.
- Utilize sage (I prefer white sage because the scent is mild) or palo santo wood (especially helpful in releasing emotional energies). These can be found at spiritual bookstores, online, or even at some natural food stores.
- You will use a lighter to light the small sage bundle, loose sage leaves, or palo santo stick on fire. You will want to use a dish of some sort beneath to prevent potential damage if sparks or debris should fall onto furniture or the floor.
- Set your intention to cleanse and clear the space of stagnant, negative, or dense energies. You can do this however you choose. Some people say a prayer prior to starting. You can call upon your spirit helpers to assist if it resonates.

183

- You may do a small area or the entire house. Walk from corner to corner of the room, creating a smoke trail. You will want to open and go into closets, go behind open doors, etc. The idea is to cover the entire perimeter of the room or house you are intending to cleanse.
- Once you have created the smoke trail through the rooms you choose to clear, leave the windows open for a while to allow the fresh air in and the negative energy out. Time will vary. I usually allow thirty minutes to an hour, depending on how smoky it got and how strong the smell of sage or palo santo remains.
- When it feels as if the process is complete and the space feels sufficiently purified, close the windows.
- This can also be done using sage or palo santo essential oils and a tissue. Simply place several drops of the oil on the tissue and wave it around as you walk the perimeter of the room, while using your intention to clear the space. This is useful as it does not smell as intense as lit leaves or wood. This technique works great when you are clearing a space that does not have windows or they do not open. For example, at the office or in a hotel room.
- You can do this process whenever you feel led to cleanse and clear a space. I recommend doing approximately once every week or two, although it can be done more or less often depending on your needs.

Clearing Stones

Another way to cleanse or raise the energetic frequency of a space is to include items of higher vibration and those which have purifying properties. These can include Himalayan salt and selenite lamps and stones, quartz crystals, amethyst crystals, and indigo gabbro crystals. These stones come from the earth and can help us connect with the powerful Mother Earth energy, which can be nurturing, healing, and cleansing.

Himalayan Salt and Selenite

Himalayan salt and selenite lamps are great because they are not only aesthetically pleasing, but they raise the vibration and cleanse the energy of a space. In the past, you could only find these at stone shops, spiritual bookstores, and metaphysical stores. Now these are common and can be found in home stores, department stores, and online. I am particularly fond of selenite as it does not have to be cleansed (some stones need to be cleared and recharged, which I will discuss soon), and it can help clear other stones. To do this, you simply put the other stones near the lamp for a few to several hours while the selenite removes negative energies they have absorbed.

Selenite wands are also a good option to raise the vibration of a space or furniture. They can be situated strategically around a room or placed under furniture to clear negative energy. I keep three long wands under the chair my therapy clients sit in and a few more under my desk. They help absorb negative energy as it is released during the healing process, which helps keep my space clear. I used to keep a few under all sides of my bed to do the same, until I found something else that I prefer.

Himalayan salt can be used in the bath to help cleanse and purify your energy field. It can be found in smaller salt crystals or large chunks, which can be put into a sheer bag and dipped into the water for a few minutes prior to or during a bath. Other salts that are beneficial include sea salt and Epsom salt. Add half a cup of salts to a bath and soak for thirty minutes in water as warm as you are comfortable.

At times, when I need some deep clearing, I also place a selenite wand at the bottom of the tub to absorb negative energies. This is powerful and works very well. Selenite does splinter, so you should be careful not to place directly on your skin and to rinse the tub of any selenite splinters or residue following the bath. I have never had a problem with this, but it is something to be aware of if you choose to use selenite in this way.

Quartz Crystals

Quartz crystals are great for clearing energy and raising the energetic vibration of yourself and/or your space. The various crystals are recognized for different strengths and functions. Quartz crystal is well-known for its healing and clearing properties. It is made of silica, which is also a component found within the human body. An alchemical reaction takes place when these stones touch the human skin causing a merging of energies that is very healing. These crystals can be placed around a room to transmute and raise energetic vibration of the room or space. I place these crystals around my office and beside my nightstand. When I need clearing or healing, I place a few on my body or hold them in each hand. Additionally, I have a few pendants and bracelets that I wear when I need extra help. They feel great and are very versatile as the color is neutral.

Amethyst Crystals

These crystals are known to be purifying, balancing, healing, and protective against negative energies. These can be great to wear, carry as a chunk in your pocket or purse, or to place within your home or office.

Rose Quartz Crystals

These crystals are known to aid the heart in healing because they emit the vibration of love and compassion. These are especially nice to wear as a pendent on a chain, near the heart chakra. Rose quartz crystals are very nurturing and help one connect with the most powerful energy in the Universe—love.

Smoky Quartz Crystals

This variety of crystal is helpful in transmuting negative energy and can help shield against negative energy. These can be worn as jewelry or placed within home or office spaces.

Shungite

Shungite absorbs negative energy and is also known to protect against electromagnetic frequencies. This is a great stone to place near your computer. I keep a shungite cube in each corner of my office to absorb negativity. I also use the combination of a shungite pyramid, a large quartz crystal and selenite wands under the chair my therapy clients sit in during sessions.

Indigo Gabbro

This is one of my favorite stones, also known as Mystic Merlanite. It transmutes negative energy, is an energy-protective stone, and helps draw in the energy that one needs. I recently ordered a pendent, which I often wear when I do public speaking. It makes a positive difference with my energy level and feels almost as if it creates a field of protection from negative energies around me. I have placed rough indigo gabbro stones around every room of my home and office spaces to clear negative energy and raise the vibration. The shift in these spaces was very noticeable upon arrival of the stones.

Create a Grid with your Stones

One of the things you can do, if you purchase and place quite a few stones around a space, is to create a high vibrational grid. Start with stones that have been cleared and recharged vibrationally (see next section). Talk with your stones about what you see their purpose to be. I know this sounds strange, but these stones are powerful and have a consciousness of their own. If you are creating a grid of stones with the intention to clear negative energy and raise the vibration of the space, you would let them know this. When I create a grid, I speak of my intention and ask that the stones connect and work together to accomplish this, as well as raise the vibration of the space. The stones you choose for this may depend on what their strengths are. I have created a grid with quartz crystals, although have found indigo gabbro stones to be more effective because they do not need to be cleared very often.

Cleansing of Stones

Most of the stones I mentioned, with the exception of selenite, need to be cleansed occasionally, to maintain their full strength and effectiveness. This can be done by rinsing the stones with water and placing them in the moonlight overnight, preferably during a full moon. You can also soak them in salt water for a while, rinse, and place in the moonlight. They can be situated around a selenite lamp, best if done overnight. I have got a routine in which I cleanse all the stones in the house monthly the night of the full moon or as close to the full moon as possible. I rinse them with water and place them outside for the entire night, in a spot where they will have as much moonlight exposure as possible. This not only clears them of negative energies, but the energy of the full moon amplifies the energy of the stones.

These stones create an energy that is healing and clearing. I use a combination of selenite, salt lamps, shungite, quartz crystals, amethyst crystals, and indigo gabbro within my office space. They help keep the space clean and clear of negative energies. My clients notice the high vibration of the office and how easy it is to go deep into their stuff while we work together.

The information I have provided is very basic and based on my personal experiences and understandings of the stones. There is a wealth of information available on the internet, in books, at stone shops, and shows if you desire to learn more. There are so many stones, not mentioned, with a variety of purposes to help you personally or within your office space.

Use of Plants to Clear Energy

Plants have been known to create a nice vibration within a space by purifying the air of chemicals and pollutants, increasing oxygen, and absorbing negative energies. By bringing about a sense of peace and improving aesthetics, they can help us feel less stressed and improve overall well-being. Some plants that are known to help include peace lily, rosemary, oregano, basil, aloe vera, orchid, jasmine, eucalyptus, cactus and succulents, bonsai money plant, bamboo, chrysanthemum, ivy, and other broad-leaved plants. This list is not all inclusive but mentions some of those I have heard about or tried over the years to improve energy within my home and office spaces. I encourage you to do additional research if you are interested in clearing energy or raising the energetic vibration within your home or office space through plant use.

High Vibrational Music

Another tool I use to create a high vibrational space is high vibrational music created and infused with certain intentions, such as inner peace and unconditional love. This music is deeply healing and assists my clients in going inward to access and process content buried within the subconscious. Some of my favorite healing music is created by gifted musicians Paradiso and Rasamayi. They utilize the instruments of crystal bowls and didgeridoos, as well as powerful and pure intentions to assist in deep healing and multidimensional evolution. I have seen them in concert several times and have purchased their CDs, which I play in the background during therapy and healing sessions. More information and music can be located at www.paradisoandrasamayi.com.

Another great source of high vibrational music is PowerThoughts Meditation Club (www.powerthoughtsmeditationclub.com). I learned about this music from a friend and yoga studio owner, Katerina. She plays their music, and other music, that uses solfeggio frequencies while she teaches yoga. This encourages healing and a deeper experience during one's yoga practice. Her son is a musician and informed her that the music is absorbed into the space, which I have since noticed that the studio has taken on the energetic vibrations of the music. I can feel and sense the higher vibrations of the music in the floor when I lie on my mat, even when it is not playing. Between the way Katerina teaches yoga (she is a true master of movement) and the vibrational music playing in the background, it makes for a unique experience. When I am finished, it feels as if I have been cleaned and cleared energetically, had a workout, experienced a massage, and been to a meditation class all in one! Playing high vibrational music is a great way to raise the vibration of a home or space while raising your energetic vibration and cleansing your energy.

According to a PowerThoughts Meditation Club blog on solfeggio frequencies, by exposing the body and mind to these frequencies, you can accomplish a better sense of balance and deep inner healing by aligning yourself with the rhythms and tones that form the basis of the Universe. The solfeggio frequencies are said to be the original frequencies used by the Gregorian monks when they chanted in meditations. Their chants, based on the six notes (396 Hz, 417 Hz, 528 Hz, 639 Hz, 741 Hz, and 852 Hz). Music with these frequencies is ideal for meditation, yoga, and relaxation. Sometimes I play this music while working or in the background when I wish to create a peaceful environment. PowerThoughts Meditation Club has both free music and some that you can purchase. Here are explanations of some solfeggio frequencies quoted directly from their Solfeggio Frequencies blog.[66]

174 Hz—The lowest of the tones appears to be a natural anesthetic. It tends to remove pain physically, energetically as well as karmic energy. 174Hz frequency gives your organs a sense of security, safety and love, motivating them to do their best.[67]

285 Hz—This tone is useful when treating wounds, cuts, burns, or any other form of dam-

[66] "Info on Solfeggio Frequencies," Power Thoughts Meditation Club, accessed June 8, 2019, http://powerthoughtsmeditationclub.com/info-on-solfeggio-frequencies/.

[67] "Info on Solfeggio Frequencies," Power Thoughts Meditation Club, accessed June 8, 2019, http://powerthoughtsmeditationclub.com/info-on-solfeggio-frequencies/.

aged tissue. 285 Hz solfeggio frequency is said to be directly connected to our body's mind and soul's blueprint for optimal health and physical well-being, due to its amazing ability to remember what should be and to return cells to its original form. It influences energy fields sending them messages to restructure damaged organ. 285 Hz is about remembering and healing you, your internal organs and your energy.[68]

396 Hz—Cleanses the feeling of guilt, which often represents one of the basic obstacles to realization, enables achievement of goals in the most direct way. It releases you from the feeling of guilt and fear by bringing down the defense mechanisms. This solfeggio frequency can also be used as a means of grounding, awakening, sobering, and returning to reality.[69]

417 Hz—Next tone from the solfeggio scale is connected with resonation process or processes of amplification. Re can "delete" person's "alienation from God" and enable returning to the "right path." This solfeggio frequency cleanses traumatic experiences and clears destructive influences of past events. It can be used for clearing limiting impressions, which disables the person to achieve her life goals. When speaking of cellular processes, tone Re encourages the cell and its DNA to function in an optimal way. [The] 417

[68] "Info on Solfeggio Frequencies," Power Thoughts Meditation Club, accessed June 8, 2019, http://powerthoughtsmeditationclub.com/info-on-solfeggio-frequencies/.

[69] n.d. *Power Thoughts Meditation Club 2019*. Accessed June 8, 2019. http://powerthoughtsmeditationclub.com/info-on-solfeggio-frequencies/.

frequency energizes your body cells and helps to use their creative potentials.[70]

528 Hz—Used to return human DNA to its original, perfect state. If it is used in a way described in Webster's dictionary, by communicating the wanted effect and with the energy support from the "light," miracles will happen! Process of DNA reparation is followed by beneficial effects—increased amount of life energy, clarity of mind, awareness, awakened or activated creativity, ecstatic states like deep inner peace, dance, and celebration. It also opens the person for deep spiritual experiences and spiritual enlightenment.[71]

639 Hz—This frequency enables creation of harmonious community and harmonious interpersonal relationships. It can be used for dealing with relationship problems—those in family, between partners, friends, or social problems. It can be used to encourage the cell to communicate with its environment. This ancient solfeggio frequency enhances communication, understanding, tolerance, and love. [The] 639 frequency can also be used for communication with parallel worlds or spiritual spheres.[72]

---

[70] "Info on Solfeggio Frequencies," Power Thoughts Meditation Club, accessed June 8, 2019, http://powerthoughtsmeditationclub. com/info-on-solfeggio-frequencies/.

[71] "Info on Solfeggio Frequencies," Power Thoughts Meditation Club, accessed June 8, 2019, http://powerthoughtsmeditationclub. com/info-on-solfeggio-frequencies/.

[72] "Info on Solfeggio Frequencies," Power Thoughts Meditation Club, accessed June 8, 2019, http://powerthoughtsmeditationclub. com/info-on-solfeggio-frequencies/.

741 Hz—Cleans the cell from the toxins. Frequent use of 741 Hz leads to a healthier, simpler life, and also to change to diet toward foods which are not poisoned by various kinds of toxins. It also cleans the cells from different kinds of electromagnetic radiations. Another important application of this sound frequency is cleansing infections—viral, bacterial, and fungal. This tone leads you to pure, stable and spiritual life.[73]

852 Hz—Solfeggio 852 Hz is directly connected to the third eye chakra and can be used as means for awakening inner strength and self-realization. It is good for dissolving stagnant mental energy from overthinking. It is said to clear up energy blockages that before have hindered clear and strong communication with our higher self, spirit guides, and spirit helpers.[74]

963 Hz—This tone awakens any system to its original, perfect state. It is concerned with the Light and all-embracing Spirit, and enables direct experience, the return to Oneness. This frequency reconnects you with Spirit, or the nonvibrational energies of the spiritual world. It will enable you to experience Oneness—our true nature.[75]

---

[73] "Info on Solfeggio Frequencies," Power Thoughts Meditation Club, accessed June 8, 2019, http://powerthoughtsmeditationclub.com/info-on-solfeggio-frequencies/.

[74] "Info on Solfeggio Frequencies," Power Thoughts Meditation Club, accessed June 8, 2019, http://powerthoughtsmeditationclub.com/info-on-solfeggio-frequencies/.

[75] "Info on Solfeggio Frequencies," Power Thoughts Meditation Club, accessed June 8, 2019, http://powerthoughtsmeditationclub.com/info-on-solfeggio-frequencies/.

Raising the Vibration through Essential Oils and Candles

Essential oils can be utilized within a space to clear the air and raise the energetic vibration. They also have a positive effect on us because they are calming and soothing and can help raise our emotional energies. They have been recognized as having healing and medicinal properties. There are countless types of essential oils, and this is not an area that I am an expert in. Some of the popular citrus scents I have heard to be mood enhancing include lemon, orange, and grapefruit. Other essential oils I have either used or known by others to be beneficial for clearing negative energy and promoting positivity include lavender, rose, sage, eucalyptus, jasmine, rosemary, clary sage, thyme, oregano, frankincense, and myrrh.

With so many known and diverse benefits and purposes, essential oils may be an area for you to explore and add to your self-care toolbox if it interests you. It would be wise to not only explore the benefits but also how to use them as some can be applied to the skin, inhaled, or diffused. Reputable oil vendors will be able to help you navigate essential oils. Additionally, you can get information by reading books and exploring the internet.

Another great way to connect spiritually to higher vibrations is through candles as they represent life energy and light. Candles have long been used within religious and spiritual rituals. They are especially powerful if used with positive intent. Even choosing specific colors, called candle color therapy, for specific purposes can increase their power. Some use candle color therapy as they do Reiki energy healing and chakra balancing—for example, choosing a white candle for peace or purification, green candles for prosperity, pink for compassion and love. The idea is that color has frequency and is very powerful to infuse your positive intentions with colors to support that which you are trying to attract or create within your life.

I usually keep a white candle burning in my office while I work to represent purification and to bring in light. Sometimes I burn candles around the house or in my office space that are scented with sage oil or lavender to clear negative energy. I am sensitive to chemicals and perfumes, so I only burn clean-burning candles made of beeswax or soy wax, scented with pure essential oils and with a cotton wick. A company that I get these products from is called Swan Creek Candle Company (www.SwanCreekCandle.com). I have also purchased clean-burning candles from the health food store. These are some things you may want to consider if you are sensitive or desire a "green" option for candle burning.

Raising the Vibration with Art

An additional method to raise the vibration of a space is to infuse it with high vibrational artwork. If you find the art to be beautiful, meaningful, and it appeals to you, it will instigate happiness when you enjoy it. People who are spiritual, religious, or both often raise the vibration of their space by adding sculptures, fountains, pictures, and tapestries that resonate with their beliefs. This could be visuals of angels, ascended masters (such as Jesus, Mother Mary, Buddha, Kwan Yin), and others. This is very personal for each individual, and these items can help you connect with your Divine by having them present in your space. This is especially helpful if you have a sacred space where you meditate or work.

Establishing Boundaries by Using the Power of Command

There are a few things I have found to be essential for myself and my clients to maintain energetic sovereignty. The first has been to do the inner work necessary regarding beliefs about personal power. This cannot be overemphasized and creates a strong foundation for personal power and energy management.

There are other energy management tools that use intention and the power of command to establish energetic boundaries prior to interacting with other people, going to work, going out in public, or into energetically challenging environments. The power of command, as defined by Rose Rosetree means the "use of command as effective speech—not shouting or begging, simply requesting. But requesting by knowing the what, where, and why of what you're requesting, while being actively connected with the Divine healing being of your choice."[76]

Some of the tools I am about to share include calling on your Divine spiritual helpers for assistance, through use of the power of command. I encourage you to read the remainder of this chapter with an open mind. If it does not resonate or fit within your belief system, feel free to discard the information, and move onto the next chapter. I feel led to share the following information as it has made a positive impact in my life and ability to work with my empathic nature.

Spirit can be a tremendous help with energy management and energy clearing if we call upon our spirit team for help. They love it when we ask for assistance and, in some cases, will not intervene unless we ask for help, as they desire to honor our free will. When we use our power of command, we ask for what we need in a way that accesses our power to cocreate with the Universe by recognizing that we have the personal power to do so. We do this by connecting with spirit (which I will explain in a moment) and asking for help in a clear and confident manner and with the belief that your request for help will be heard and honored. I will give some examples of how to use the power of command, but you may choose not to use the scripts that I provide and come up with some that resonate with you and your belief system. These are my scripts, which have elements of what I have learned from Rosetree's book and through healing work with YaMaEl Cash through www.divinitycodes.com.

I often begin my power of command statements with "I call upon my powerful I Am presence…" By doing this, I am asking to connect with my higher self, higher consciousness, Universal consciousness, God consciousness, part of me that is part of God, and all that is.[77]

---

[76] Rose Rosetree, *Use Your Power of Command for Spiritual Cleansing and Protection* (Sterling: Women's Intuition Worldwide, 2012), 14.

[77] Y Cash, "Divinity Code Connect to Your Divine Self," https://www.divinity-codes.com/. 4/15/18

Connect with Your Divine

A simple way to connect with your personal Divine is to close your eyes, intend to connect (to whoever or whatever), and take three deep breaths (more if you feel three is not enough) by inhaling through your nose and exhaling out through your mouth. State out loud who you are calling upon and what you need help with. As previously mentioned, do so with the belief that you will be heard and assisted. And as you call upon your spirit team, do so in a confident voice. Below are some power-of-command statements that I use often for various purposes. Feel free to try these or come up with personal statements that you prefer.[78]

Privacy and Protection

I use this statement prior to beginning work with a client, when I go out in public, or anytime I feel I need help with energetic sovereignty, privacy, and protection.

> I call upon my powerful I Am presence to increase my energetic sovereignty, spiritual privacy, and protection to be absolutely and infinitely effective. Thank you, it is done![79]

Aura Strengthening

I use this statement to increase my energetic sovereignty and strengthen my aura several times a day...between clients, prior to each public location I visit, etc.

> I call upon my powerful I Am presence to close my aura to all but my higher self and the high-

---

[78] Rose Rosetree, *Use Your Power of Command for Spiritual Cleansing and Protection* (Sterling: Women's Intuition Worldwide, 2012), 26.

[79] Y Cash, "Divinity Code Connect to Your Divine Self," https://www.divinity-codes.com/. 4/15/18

est vibrational lightworkers (or beings) with me by choice of my soul through all time, space and dimensions.[80]

With this statement, I also zip up my energy with my intention and a hand gesture. Taking my hand from the root chakra area on the front of my body, up the center of my body, over my head to the base of my neck on the back of my body.[81]

Send Heart-Healing Energy

I learned this technique from Dr. Michael Ulm and Dr. Ellen Valentine-Laperriere through their All Light Ministries Healing Miracles Workshop. We often spend time with people who are desiring to have some of our energy, whether they realize it or not. By sending our loving energy to people who we will be interacting with in advance, they will not have the need to draw it from us. Imagine that you have one hundred units of unconditional love each day when you wake up. Intend that you send a small fraction (like a half or one unit of love) of this love to the people you will be interacting with prior to seeing them—basically sending your love ahead. This is a kind and compassionate gesture you are offering the person, and it helps to prevent unwanted draws upon your energy. Here is how it's done.

With the fingers of your right hand, brush toward your heart from right to center and below the heart to center. With the fingers of your left hand, brush toward your heart from left to center and from above the heart to center.

Grow the heart energy of love in your hands (rub them together, then hold them apart, toward each other, and sense the growing love between your palms. With the intention to send unconditional love energy to the person (I usually send a half or one unit of my uncon-

---

[80] Y Cash, "Divinity Code Connect to Your Divine Self," https://www.divinity-codes.com/. 4/15/18

[81] Michael L. Ulm and Ellen R. Valentine-Laperriere, *All Light Ministries Healing Miracles Workshop Manual* (Charlotte: All Light Ministries, 2018), 27.

ditional love) and ask the Divine to infuse it with whatever love and light he/she needs. Then send it to the person by gently blowing it your open hands metaphorically toward them, as if they are standing in front of you. Do three times.[82]

Space-Clearing Commands

I use the statements below to ask for assistance from my spiritual helpers to clear the space within my home or office of negative and lower vibrations.

> I call upon the highest vibrational spirit helpers who love me unconditionally and are with me by choice of my soul. (You can call upon God, specific ascended masters, archangels, etc. if you prefer). Please join me now and create a protective and healing circle of pure golden light around me.
>
> I call upon my powerful I Am Presence and the spirit helpers who love me unconditionally and are with me by choice of my soul to clean and clear every layer and level of this space (be specific— home, office, vehicle, etc.) of any and all negative and discordant energies and entities. Please transmute all negative energies and entities into the light leaving my space free of all negativity, dense, and stuck or stagnant energy, thought forms, draining cords, and unwanted fragments of any kind.
>
> I ask that you now fill my space with the highest vibrations of peace, unconditional love, light, and joy. Thank you! It is done.[83]

---

[82] Michael L. Ulm and Ellen R. Valentine-Laperriere, *All Light Ministries Healing Miracles Workshop Manual* (Charlotte: All Light Ministries, 2018),p. 5.

[83] Y. Cash, "Divinity Code Connect to Your Divine Self," https://www.divinity-codes.com/. 4/15/18

Following the command, leave time for the work to be done and trust that it is so. You can repeat after a while if you feel it is necessary (I would wait at least an hour).

Personal Clearing Command

> I call upon the highest vibrational spirit helpers who love me unconditionally and are with me by choice of my soul. (You can call upon God, specific ascended masters, archangels, etc. if you prefer) Please join me now and create a protective and healing circle of pure golden light around me.
>
> I call upon my powerful I Am presence and the spirit helpers who love me unconditionally and are with me by choice of my soul to clean and clear every layer and level of my entire physical body, subtle bodies, and spaces between my subtle bodies. Please remove any and all negative and discordant energies and entities. Please locate, cut, and dissolve all cords of attachment that are not for my highest good. Please transmute all negative energies and entities into the light leaving me free of negativity, thought forms, hooks, cords of attachments and fragments of any kind through all time, space, and dimensions.
>
> I ask that you now fill me highest vibrations of peace, unconditional love, and light.
>
> Thank you! It is done."[84]

Following the command, leave time for the work to be done and trust that it is so. You can repeat after a while if you feel it is necessary (I would wait at least an hour).

---

[84] Y. Cash, "Divinity Code Connect to Your Divine Self," https://www.divinity-codes.com/. 4/15/18

Healing Stream of Grace

I learned a tool that I use often from Cyndi Dale's book called *Energetic Boundaries*. It utilizes the power of command to quickly replace negative cords of attachment between people with a healing stream of grace. Additionally, it resets energetic boundaries to allow only for higher vibrations in the energetic field. Use the following commands to ask for assistance:

1. I ask the Divine to substitute a healing stream of grace for all active cords and contracts that are affecting me adversely.
2. I accept the stream of grace with the understanding that it is perfect for me. (Feel for the acceptance within you.)
3. I ask the Divine to cleanse me of any remnants or effects of the cord and contract.
4. I ask the Divine to provide a healing stream of grace for all others concerned in this cord or contract.
5. I ask the Divine to now heal me internally and to restore my energetic boundaries so I can now live freely and in harmony with the Divine will.
6. Feel gratitude for the Divine assistance received and the life change that resulted.

Following this healing, you can state these intentions out loud or in your mind.

> I am surrounded by a living and unconditional Universal field (the energetic field of the Divine).
> My energetic boundaries only allow the vibrations of love or above in and deflect or transmute all negative energies.[85]

---

[85] Cyndi Dale, *Energetic Boundaries* (Boulder: Sounds True Publishing, 2011), 65–66.

Surround Yourself in Light

Another tool that can be helpful is to imagine or visualize surrounding yourself in a column of protective white, gold, purple, light pink, or blue light that extends down to the core of the earth and up into the heavens. White light is associated with positivity and can be called upon for healing and protection from negative energies. Gold energy is considered one of the strongest colors for protecting from negative energies and is associated with Christ consciousness. Purple light protects against negativity and ushers in Divine guidance. Light pink exudes the energy of compassion and can be protective. It allows us to radiate the Divine Feminine compassion outward yet protects us from being drained by others as we are empathetic and compassionate. Blue light is the color associated with the protection of Archangel Michael and represents protection, courage, and strength.

EMF Protection

Some people are sensitive to electromagnetic frequencies emitted through electronic devices including cell phones, tablets, laptops, televisions, headphones and others. An option to enhance and protect your energy field from EMF includes wearing jewelry specifically designed to minimize the potential negative effects. Energetically sensitive people can also benefit from adding sacred geometry holograms to their phones, personal computers, tablets, televisions, vehicles, and homes to minimize electromagnetic waves and radio frequencies. Other products that can be helpful to protect against EMF radiation include laptop shields, protective cell phone/tablet cases, and specially designed earbuds/headphones. Benefits can include improved sleep quality, concentration, and vitality. Websites that I have ordered from are www.sovereign-alliance.com, www.harmonipendant.com, and www.defendershield.com, although there are many vendors of EMF protection on the internet.

Summary

The proper flow and balance of life energies is essential for optimal health and well-being. This is true within our physical bodies, within our energy field, and the energy of the spaces in which we reside. Energy management and clearing is an aspect of self-care that people often overlook, yet it can make a tremendous impact on your energy and the way you feel. It is especially useful for people who are highly empathic or sensitive. Many concepts and ideas have been shared within this chapter, including understanding energy, energy centers and the aura, empaths, energy vampires, personal power, grounding, and creating high vibrational spaces. Some methods to raise the energetic frequency of home and offices spaces include smudging, use of clearing stones and crystals, energy-clearing plants, high vibrational music, and essential oils and candles. We also explored use of the power of command to connect with your Divine, increase energetic privacy and protection, aura strengthening, sending heart-healing energy, clear spaces, and personal energy cleansing, and setting energetic boundaries. These methods, combined with other self-care recommendations shared in previous chapters, boost resiliency and help you function at your personal best.

CHAPTER 10

Self-Care Strategy

**If your compassion does not
include yourself,
it is incomplete.**
—Buddha
(Goodreads.com)

Hopefully, the reading to this point has stimulated some ideas regarding your self-care regimen. Now it is time for the rubber to meet the road—to take action toward your intended goal of better self-care. Many suggestions have been offered, but the important thing here is that you get in touch with what self-care looks like for you. It is going to be different for each person as we must take our interests and constitutions into consideration. For example, one person might most enjoy beginning the day slowly with yoga and a gentle meditation, and another may enjoy an early morning rigorous workout at the gym. And it is possible that exercise is not enjoyable in the morning and is saved for much later in the day. There is no right or wrong to this, just find what works best for you.

Awareness Regarding Obstacles

It is important to have awareness regarding any obstacles you have to self-care and a willingness to work through these. If you do not value yourself or believe that you are worth it, it will be more difficult to commit to the time and nurturing that self-care will require. In this instance, doing some things to get yourself out of the way may be necessary. For example, doing daily affirmations or visiting a therapist to do subconscious-belief repatterning.

If the obstacle is time, you may have to reprioritize and create some openings within your schedule to care for your needs. If you do not have the proper equipment, you may need to make an investment. Examples include purchasing a bicycle, rebounder, weights, athletic shoes and/or clothing, membership to a gym or yoga studio, juicer, sea salt, music, therapy sessions, a journal, cooking supplies, detoxifying tea, etc.

Self-Care Self-Assessment

It is helpful to take an inventory to get a baseline regarding where you currently are regarding self-care. I encourage you to take a gentle and nonjudgmental approach with this. Meet yourself where you are, like you would do with someone you really care about, taking an honest look at how you are feeling, what you are doing, what is going well, and what is not going well.

Here are some questions to ponder which may get you thinking about how to approach your self-care. Asking yourself questions will help you get clarity regarding how things are going currently and the direction you would like to take your self-care.

- What does self-care look like to me?
- How do I feel about committing time and energy to myself for self-care?
- How can I be kinder and more gentle with myself?
- How can I make my life easier?
- What activities and habits can I release in order to make more room for my self-care?

205

- Which habits and activities help me the most?
- What am I doing that is working well?
- What are the obstacles that prevent me from taking better care of myself?
- How do I talk to myself (internal dialogue)? Is my self-talk positive or negative?
- What do I need? How can I meet my needs?
- What activities do I enjoy that refresh me?
- How can I get off to a better start each day?
- What gets me really relaxed before I sleep each night?
- Which foods make me feel the best and give me the most energy?
- What motivates and inspires me to take better care of myself?

Included below is a self-assessment with self-scoring to bring awareness and to help you identify areas to focus on. This scale was developed by Lyle Miller and Alma Dell Smith of Boston Medical Center, and the activity was created by Figley Institute for self-care planning purposes.

How Vulnerable Are You to Stress?[86]

Instructions: Rate each item from 1 (always) to 5 (never), according to how much of the time the statement is true of you. Be sure to mark each item, even if it does not apply to you—for example, if you don't smoke, circle 1 next to item six.

	Always		Sometimes		Never
1. I eat at least one hot, balanced meal a day.	1	2	3	4	5
2. I get 7–8 hours of sleep at least four nights a week.	1	2	3	4	5

---

[86] Charles R. Figley, *Counterbalance the Intensity of Your Work: Compassion Stress Management Participant Workbook* (Tallassee: Figley Institute, 2013), 14–15.

3. I give and receive affection regularly.   1   2   3   4   5

4. I have at least one relative within 50 miles, on whom I can rely.   1   2   3   4   5

5. I exercise to the point of perspiration at least twice a week.   1   2   3   4   5

6. I limit myself to less than half a pack of cigarettes a day.   1   2   3   4   5

7. I take fewer than five alcohol drinks a week.   1   2   3   4   5

8. I am the appropriate weight for my height.   1   2   3   4   5

9. I have an income adequate to meet basic expenses.   1   2   3   4   5

10. I get strength from my religious beliefs.   1   2   3   4   5

11. I regularly attend club or social activities.   1   2   3   4   5

12. I have a network of friends and acquaintances.   1   2   3   4   5

13. I have one or more friends to confide in about personal matters.   1   2   3   4   5

14. I am in good health (including eyesight, hearing, and teeth).   1   2   3   4   5

15. I am able to speak openly about my feelings when angry or worried.   1   2   3   4   5

16. I have regular conversations with the people I live with about domestic problems—for example, chores and money.   1   2   3   4   5

17. I do something for fun at least once a week.	1	2	3	4	5
18. I am able to organize my time effectively.	1	2	3	4	5
19. I drink fewer than three cups of coffee (or other caffeine-rich drinks) a day.	1	2	3	4	5
20. I take some quiet time for myself during the day.	1	2	3	4	5

1 = Always
2 = Often
3 = Sometimes
4 = Rarely
5 = Never

Scoring Instructions

Scoring Instructions:

To calculate your score, add up the figures and subtract 20.

Total score _____ - 20 = _____

Score Interpretation:

✓ A score **below 10** indicates **excellent resistance** to stress.
✓ A score **over 30** indicates **some vulnerability** to stress;
✓ A score **over 50** indicates **serious vulnerability** to stress.

If your score falls between defined ranges, use the defined range closest to your score when you enter it on your Score Pattern Analysis worksheet.

When creating your Self-care Plan

◆ Notice that nearly all the items describe situations and behaviors over which you have a great deal of control.
◆ Review the items on which you scored three or higher.
◆ Consider those items for your self-care plan.
◆ Concentrate first on those that are easiest to change—for example, eating a hot, balanced meal daily and having fun at least once a week—before tackling those that seem more difficult.
◆ If useful, fine tune your results using the table below.
◆ Remember to celebrate your accomplishments along the way!

To fine tune awareness of your areas of strength and vulnerability, average the scores for items as indicated below. You may choose to focus your self-care goals on areas in which average scores equal 3 or higher.

Category	Items	Average Score
Rest and Exercise	2 5 20	
Finances and Time Management	9 18	
Leisure & Lifestyle	10 11 17	
Social Support & Communication	3 4 12 13 15 16	
Nutrition	1 7 19	
Health & Fitness	6 8 14	

Empower Yourself

Empowerment requires us to take full responsibility for ourselves, our choices, our actions, and our lives. This is especially important as it relates to self-care because only you can do it. To do this, we must get in touch with and live according to our own values. What do we cherish and wish to create related to our health and well-being? For example, I know some people who enjoy eating whatever they want in the moment and indulgent drinking each weekend. They desire to live for the moment, yet they complain about not feeling and looking as well as they would like. Some prefer to engage in excellent self-care as a lifestyle. These people tend to feel great, have a lot of energy, and look younger than their actual age.

Those opting for adopting excellent self-care habits may value living a longer life with fewer health challenges.

It is helpful to live according to your own inner guidance system of feelings, beliefs, and expectations of yourself rather than adopting those of others. When we take full responsibility for ourselves, we can no longer blame our failures and disappointments on others. We find the security in ourselves rather than seeking it from those around us. This is how we claim our personal power and freedom, leading to more fulfilling lives.

Empowerment is very important as it relates to self-care because self-care is something you can do for yourself to make your life better. It requires self-awareness, authenticity, personal leadership, commitment, belief, and trust in yourself.

> *As soon as you trust yourself, you will know how to live.*
> **—Johann Wolfgang von Goethe**
> (Goodreads.com.)

Sometimes we learn to trust ourselves through trial and error, but the lessons learned are invaluable, so be willing to try new things and take risks.

When we empower ourselves, we create our reality by making positive choices and changes through our intentions, thoughts, actions, words, and beliefs. These choices all hold a vibration and ripple out into the world, drawing your reality to you. This vibration also increases the positive effect you have on others when you feel good within and about yourself. These are sound reasons to keep things positive and to work on removing negativity from within yourself and your life rather than living by chance. We take initiative rather than waiting for things to happen and becoming a victim of circumstance.

This may require you to stretch yourself and step outside your comfort zone. You can reach your full potential by acknowledging and facing your fears and insecurities. Become aware of how you sabotage yourself, your limiting beliefs, codependencies on other people and take responsibility for yourself and allow others to do the same. This is when the greatest growth occurs. By facing your fear and doing it anyway, you gain strength and courage.

You can become the most brilliant version of yourself and live the life of your dreams. It begins with the choice to do so. It does require work, especially inner work. There are no shortcuts, miracle pills, or magic wands as many would prefer. It is a journey like no other, complete with challenges, learning, and unfoldment beyond what one can imagine. Self-care is the foundation and is necessary to going deeper into love and ascension.

Self-care is an act of self-love. When you understand your value, accept, and appreciate yourself, you will more easily maintain self-care practices with consistency. When you are deeply committed to self-care, it can become as natural as breathing and something that is infused in and throughout each day. It becomes a way of living…one in which you would not consider harming or sacrificing yourself any more than you would consider harming another.

Self-Care Commitment

You yourself, as much as anyone in the entire Universe, deserve your love and affection.
—Buddha
(Medium.com)

An integral aspect to successfully incorporating self-care into your life or strengthening your current self-care practices is commitment. Dedicating time and resources to yourself and following through with consistent actions will ensure the success of a self-care plan. In other words, say what you are going to do and follow through. It is easy to do this with others, as they often hold us accountable, but not always easy to do with one's self.

You may find it easier to honor your commitment of self-care if you verbally speak your plan to another or others. For example, informing your spouse, best friend, close coworker, or another/others of your plans and progress on your goals. It might also be interesting to see how the perceptions of those you trust relative to your self-care compare with your self-assessment. It may be helpful to have an accountability buddy who joins you in some of your self-care, for example a running mate. If it helps you to do it with someone, by all means find another person with similar interests and have fun with it. Certainly, you will not be able to do all your self-care with someone, and you do not want to get into a situation where whether or not you do self-care is dependent on another.

There are some people who are self-motivated and would prefer full accountability because discussing or doing self-care with another would slow them down. Only you know what motivates you and works best for you.

Create a Self-Care Strategy

Now that you have read the book, pondered some questions, and done self-assessments, hopefully, you have some ideas of things you can do to improve your self-care. It is time to set some goals for your self-care. I encourage you to create SMART goals—goals that are specific, measurable, attainable, realistic, and time-based. An example of a SMART goal is, I plan to attend yoga class from 8:30 a.m. to 10:00 a.m. every Tuesday, Thursday, and either Saturday or Sunday beginning this week through August 31 of this year.

A way to measure this would be to put a star on your calendar each day you attend yoga class. Time-based goals have a beginning and ending point. This is important because it helps to make them more realistic. And there are times of the year where a goal is more achievable than other times. For example, I like to walk almost every day during the spring, summer, and fall months. However, it is not as likely or reasonable that I could walk outside this often during the winter months. So my walking goal is to walk five to six days a week from April through November and three to four days a week during the winter months.

You can also substitute self-care activities during times you are not in your regular routine. For example, I might substitute swimming or hiking for my walk or yoga class while I am on vacation. While on a business trip with a tight itinerary, I might do some gentle stretching and jogging in place in my hotel room rather than walking or attending a yoga class.

It is important to recognize that progress is the goal, not perfection. If you are not able to meet your goals for one reason or another—examples include illness, travel, and unexpected events—there is no reason to beat yourself up. Pick it up where you left off when the time is right.

Once you identify several SMART goals, it is helpful to write these down somewhere that you can see them or easily access them. These goals can be maintenance goals, which are self-care activities that you are already doing, and they are going well. The goals can be growth goals, which are goals that are new or different from what you have already been doing. These goals are likely to stretch you a bit as they may be new. A mixture of both is helpful, however you can do what makes sense. If self-care is new to you, they may all be growth goals. Below is the self-care goal worksheet developed by Figley Institute. This may help you get started. It has space for three goals, although you can set as many as you would like.

Self-Care Goal Worksheet[87]

1. Analyze the data and compare that with self-perceptions, and the perceptions of family, friends, and colleagues.

[87] Charles R. Figley, *Counterbalance the Intensity of Your Work: Compassion Stress Management Participant Workbook* (Tallahassee: Figley Institute, 2013), 36.

2. Based on your Score Pattern Analysis, identify three (3) SMART goals which will maintain or increase your resilience to stressors. Goals may be Maintenance (continue doing what works) and/or growth (add that which will increase resilience).

3. Identify two (2) accountability buddies with whom you will meet to monitor your goals and set a time/place to meet. One buddy should be identified from your professional environment and the second should be identified from your personal life.

S-M-A-R-T
Specific—Measurable—Attainable—Realistic—Time-Based

SMART Goals	Maintenance	Growth
1.		
2.		
3.		

Are there obstacles or resistances to achieving your goals? ( ) Yes ( ) No

If yes, what are they? List here and share with your accountability buddy.

What strategies might you use to overcome the obstacles/resistances? List here and share with your accountability buddy.

Identify Buddies	Meeting Date/Time
Personal:	
Professional:	

Evaluate your plan at appropriate intervals for yourself, which can be weekly, monthly, and yearly. You can do this by yourself or with an accountability buddy. It is important to keep your plan current and to switch it up when necessary.

The plan is a guideline but is not necessary if your commitment and practice of self-care is so ingrained that it has become a lifestyle. Those who have reached this point with their self-care are able to acknowledge their needs and flow with them regardless of what is going on in their lives. This is the ultimate goal.

Summary

Self-care is very empowering as only you can do it for yourself. It requires acknowledging, owning, and providing for your needs and nurturing. It is helpful to have an awareness regarding any obstacles that have kept you from meeting your goals and having a plan to overcome them. We can gain awareness by asking ourselves the questions outlined in the chapter and by completing self-assessments regarding self-care. Making a commitment to one's self to engage in healthy and mindful practice is essential. Creating a self-care strategy, which includes maintenance and growth goals is recommended. For maximum benefits, these goals should be SMART goals (specific, measurable, achievable, realistic, and time-specific).

Appendix

Recommended Reading

Awareness

I, Reality and Subjectivity by David R. Hawkins
Power vs. Force: The Hidden Determinants of Human Behavior by David R. Hawkins
The Eye of the I by David R. Hawkins
The Four Agreements by Don Miguel Ruiz
The New Earth by Eckhart Tolle
The Power of Now by Eckhart Tolle

Beliefs

The Biology of Belief by Bruce Lipton, PhD
The Hidden Messages in Water by Masaru Emoto
The Power by Rhonda Byrne
The Spontaneous Healing of Belief by Gregg Braden
You Can Heal Your Life by Louise Hay

Compassion

A Year of Living with More Compassion: 52 Quotes & Weekly Compassion Practices by Richard Fields, PhD, Editor
Self-Compassion: The Proven Power of Being Kind to Yourself by Kristin Neff, PhD

The Mindful Self-Compassion Workbook: A Proven Way to Accept Yourself, Build Inner Strength, and Thrive by Kristin Neff, PhD and Christopher Germer, PhD

Energy Management

Energetic Boundaries by Cyndi Dale
Energy Medicine: Balancing Your Body's Energies for Optimal Health, Joy, and Vitality by Donna Eden and David Feinstein
Positive Energy by Judith Orloff, MD
The Empath's Survival Guide: Life Strategies for Sensitive People by Judith Orloff, MD
The Highly Sensitive Person: How to Thrive When the World Overwhelms You by Elaine Aron, PhD

Intuition

The Psychic Pathway by Sonia Choquette
Trust Your Vibes by Sonia Choquette
Your Sixth Sense: Unlocking the Power of Your Intuition by Belleruth Naparstek

Mindfulness

A Year of Living Mindfully: 52 Quotes and Weekly Mindfulness Practices by Richard Fields, PhD, Editor
Be Here Now by Ram Dass
Full Catastrophe Living by Jon Kabat-Zinn, PhD
Wherever You Go, There You Are by Jon Kabat-Zinn, PhD

Parenting

Parenting from the Inside Out by Daniel Siegel, MD and Mary Hartzell, MEd
Raising an Emotionally Intelligent Child: The Heart of Parenting by John Gottman, PhD

Soul to Soul Parenting by Annie Burnside
The Highly Sensitive Child: Helping Our Children Thrive When the World Overwhelms Them by Elaine Aron, PhD

Relationships

Getting the Love You Want by Harville Hendrix, PhD
Passionate Marriage by David Schnarch, PhD
The Dance of Connection by Harriet Lerner, PhD

Trauma

In an Unspoken Voice by Peter A. Levine, PhD
The Emotion Code by Dr. Bradley Nelson
Trauma Stewardship by Laura van Dernoot Lipsky
Waking the Tiger: Healing Trauma by Peter A. Levine, PhD
Walking Your Blues Away: How to Heal the Mind and Create Emotional Well-Being by Thom Hartmann
Will I Ever Be Good Enough: Healing the Daughters of Narcissistic Mothers by Karyl McBride, PhD

Spiritual

I Am the Word channeled by Peter Selig
The Book of Love and Creation channeled by Peter Selig
The End of Your World by Adyashanti
The Isaiah Effect: Decoding the Lost Science of Prayer and Prophecy by Gregg Braden
The Seat of the Soul by Gary Zukav
Transcending the Maya Matrix Using the Seven Simple Steps: Our Innate Guide to Co-Creation and Self-Realization by Omar Makram
When Things Fall Apart: Heart Advice for Difficult Times by Pema Chodron

Wellness

Enter the Zone: A Dietary Road Map by Barry Sears, PhD

Full Catastrophe Living by Jon Kabat-Zinn, PhD

It Just Makes Sense: 7 Principles for a Joyful and Stress-Free Life by Kym Coco and Stephen Thompson

Integral Health: The Path to Human Flourishing by Elliott Dacher, MD

Robust Vitality by Julian DeVoe

Bibliography

American Institute of Stress Staff. *American Institute of Stress.* 1998. Accessed June 26, 2019.

Atkins, Robert. *How Does a Low Carb Diet Work?* Accessed June 24, 2019. https://www.atkins.com/how-it-works.

Baranowsky, Anna B. "Compassion Fatigue Specialist (Therapist) Course." Accessed February 25, 2015. https://www.ticlearn.com/.

Block, J. and A. M. Kremen. "IQ and Ego—Resiliency: Conceptual and Empirical Connections and Separateness." *Journal of Personality Social Psychology* 70, no. 2 (1996): 349–361.

Cann, Arnie, Lawrence G. Calhoun, Richard G. Tedeschi, Kanako Taku, Tanya Vishnevsky, Kelli N. Triplett, and Suzanne C. Danhauer. "A Short Form of the Posttraumatic Growth Inventory." *Anxiety, Stress & Coping* 23, no. 2 (2010). 127–137.

Cash, Y. "Divinity Code Connect to Your Divine Self." https://www.Divinitycodes.com/. 4/15/18

Dale, Cyndi. *Energetic Boundaries.* Boulder: Sounds True Publishing, 2011.

"Disease." Google. June 26, 2019. https://www.google.com/search?client=firefox-b-1-d&q=google+definitions+disease.

Einstein, Albert. "Everything Is Energy." Quote from QuoteInvestigator.com. Accessed July 8, 2019. https://quotein-vestigator.com/2012/05/16/everything-energy/.

Environmental Working Group (EWG) Staff. "EWG's Dirty Dozen for 2019." June 24, 2019. https://www.ewg.org/foodnews/summary.php.

Figley, Charles R. *Encyclopedia of Trauma: An Interdisciplinary Guide.* Newbury Park: Sage Publications, 2012.

—"Compassion Fatigue: An Expert Interview with Charles R. Figley." Interview by Jessica Gould. October 17, 2005. Accessed April 15, 2014. https://www.medscape.com/viewarticle/513615.

—. *Counterbalance the Intensity of Your Work: Compassion Stress Management Participant Workbook*. Tallahassee: Figley Institute, 2013.

Fondlin, Michelle. "What is a Chakra?" October 8, 2019. https://chopra.com/articles/what-is-a-chakra.

Gokhan, N., E. Meehan, and K. Peters. "The Value of Mindfulness-Based Methods in Teaching at a Clinical Field Placemen." *Psychological Reports* 106, no. 2 (2010): 455–466.

Green Cross Academy of Traumatology Staff. "Standards of Care." Accessed July 24, 2020. https://greencross.org/about-standards-of-care-guidelines.

Hay, Louise. "What Is Mirror Work?" Accessed July 8, 2019. https://www.louisehay.com/what-is-mirror-work/.

Hill, Ansley. "16 Superfoods That Are Worthy of the Title." July 9, 2018. Accessed June 24, 2019. https://www.healthline.com/nutrition/true-superfoods.

Holmes, T. H. and R. H. Rahe. "The Social Readjustment Rating Scale." *Journal of Psychosomatic Research* 11, no. 2 (1967): 213–221.

"Info on Solfeggio Frequencies." Power Thoughts Meditation Club. Accessed June 8, 2019. http://powerthoughtsmeditationclub.com/info-on-solfeggio-frequencies/.

Kabat-Zinn, Jon. *Full Catastrophe Living*. New York: Bantam Books, 2013.

Kluger, Jeffrey. "How Well Are You Really?" *New York Times* Special Edition on Wellness, February 15, 2019.

Lambert, Brent. "MRI Study Proving Meditation Literally Rebuilds the Brain's Gray Matter in 8 Weeks." November 11, 2014. Accessed August 1, 2020. https://www.feelguide.com/2014/11/19/harvard-unveils-mri-study-proving-meditation-literally-rebuilds-the-brains-gray-matter-in-8-weeks/.

Malone, Peggy. "Eat Less Crap, Eat More Food." Dr. Peggy Malone.com. October 10, 2013. Accessed July 25, 2020. https://drpeggymalone.com/eat-crap-eat-food/.

Marshall, Lisa. "Keto's Fans Boost Controversial Diet's Profile." July 9, 2018. Accessed June 24, 2019. https://www.webmd.com/diet/news/20180709/ketos-fans-boost-controversial-diets-profile.

Mayo Clinic Staff. "Gluten Free Diet." Mayo Clinic. Accessed June 24, 2019. https://www.mayoclinic.org/healthy-life-style/nutrition-and-healthy-eating/in-depth/gluten-free-diet/art-20048530.

—. "Glycemic Index Diet: What's Behind the Claims." Mayo Clinic. Accessed June 24, 2019. https://www.mayoclinic.org/healthy-lifestyle/nutrition-and-healthy-eating/in-depth/glycemic-index-diet/art-20048478.

—. "Healthy Lifestyle, Nutrition, and Healthy Eating." Mayo Clinic. June 24, 2019. https://www.mayoclinic.org/healthy-lifestyle/nutrition-and-healthy-eating/in-depth/mediterranean-diet/art.

—. "Paleo Diet: What Is It, and Why Is It so Popular?" Mayo Clinic. Accessed June 24, 2019. https://www.mayoclinic.org/healthy-lifestyle/nutrition-and-healthy-eating/in-depth/paleo-diet/art-20111182.

McLeod, Saul. "Maslow's Hierarchy of Needs." March 20, 2020. Accessed August 2020. https://www.simplypsychology.org/maslow.html.

Neff, Kristin. "The Three Elements of Self-Compassion." Self-Compassion.org. Accessed August 15, 2020. https://self-compassion.org/the-three-elements-of-self-compassion-2/.

Newell, Jason M. and Gordon A. MacNeil. "Professional Burnout, Vicarious Trauma, Secondary Traumatic Stress, and Compassion Fatigue: A Review of Theoretical Terms, Risk Factors, and Preventative Methods for Clinicians and Researchers." *Best Practices in Mental Health* 6, no. 2 (2010): 57–68.

Orloff, Judith. *The Empath's Survival Guide.* Boulder: Sounds True Publishing, 2017.

—. "The Top 10 Traits of an Empath." DrJudithOrloff.com. June 24, 2019. https://drjudithorloff.com/top-10-traits-of-an-empath/.

Panos, Angelea. "Understanding and Preventing Compassion Fatigue—A Handout for Professionals." Retrieved July 24, 2020 from Gift from Within—PTSD Resources for Survivors and Caregivers. July 25, 2007. Accessed June 24, 2019. http://www.giftfromwithin.org/html/prvntcf.html.

Psychology Today Staff. "Epigenetics." *Psychology Today.* Accessed June 24, 2014. https://www.psychologytoday.com/us/basics/epigenetics.

Radey, Melissa and C. R. Figley. "The Social Psychology of Compassion." *Clinical Social Work Journal,* 35 no. 1 (2007): 207–214.

Rosetree, Rose. *Use Your Power of Command for Spiritual Cleansing and Protection.* Sterling: Women's Intuition Worldwide, 2012.

Sack, David. "Nature's Antidepressant: The Dog." *Psychology Today.* June 15, 2015. Accessed June 26, 2019. https://www.psychologytoday.com/us/blog/where-science-meets-the-steps/201506/nature-s-antidepressant-the-dog.

Sears, Barry. *Mastering the Zone.* New York: HarperCollins Publishers, 1997.

Stamm, B. Hudnall. "Professional Quality of Life: Compassion Satisfaction and Fatigue Subscales, R-IV." 2009–2012. Accessed July 24, 2020. http://www.proqol.org/ProQol.

Ulm, Michael L., and Ellen R. Valentine-Laperriere. *All Light Ministries Healing Miracles Workshop Manual.* Charlotte: All Light Ministries, 2018.

Watson, Stephanie. "The Blood Type Diet." WebMD. Accessed June 24, 2019. https://www.webmd.com/diet/a-z/blood-type-diet.

WebMD Staff. "What's a Ketogenic Diet?" WebMD. Accessed June 24, 2019. https://www.webmd.com/diet/ss/slideshow-ketogenic-diet.

About the Author

Rev. Suzie DeVaughn, LMSW is the founder and CEO of Self-Care Specialists. Suzie facilitates stress management and mindfulness courses for professional caregivers and business professionals. She practices psychotherapy within her private practice in the state of Kansas. Suzie has given hundreds of informational and inspirational presentations and workshops on self-care and related topics. She has shared her expertise through blogs, podcasts, individual therapy, and healing sessions. Suzie is also the founder and owner of Blossoming Heart Center through which she facilitates energy healing, meditations, psychospiritual workshops, and retreats as an ordained minister of healing.

Suzie's education includes a master's degree in social work from Wichita State University and a bachelor's degree in organizational communications from the University of Kansas. She holds Compassion Fatigue Educator and Compassion Fatigue Therapist certifications through the Green Cross Academy of Traumatology. Her progressive therapy modalities include Hakomi body-centered psychotherapy, Psych K (subconscious belief repatterning), EMDR (Eye Movement Desensitization reprocessing), and NET (Neuro-Emotional Technique).

In addition to professional training and experience, Suzie has proficiency in self-care techniques and mindful living as the result of personal life experiences. Over two decades ago, at the age of twenty-six, she was exposed to arsenic and suffered from a variety of health problems caused by the toxicity. She was told by her doctors that it would take a miracle to heal from the exposure and the damage that it caused. Due to lifestyle changes, the power of her belief, assistance from talented holistic healers, and a strong commitment to self-care, she has made a full recovery and is in excellent health. Suzie has a passion and calling to serve those who desire to improve upon their current self-care to improve the quality of life for themselves and the people they impact.

www.selfcarespecialists.com
www.blossomingheartcenter.com

CPSIA information can be obtained
at www.ICGtesting.com
Printed in the USA
LVHW090056080821
694462LV00001B/14